had a
glass

had a glass

TOP **100** WINES FOR **2006**
UNDER **$20**

Kenji Hodgson | James Nevison

whitecap

Edited by Elaine Jones
Copyedited by Ben D'Andrea
Proofread by Joan Tetrault
Cover design and wine icons by Five Seventeen
Interior design and illustrations by Jacqui Thomas
Photoshop wizardry by Diane Yee
Photography by James Nevison and Kenji Hodgson

Printed and bound in Canada by Friesens

LIBRARY AND ARCHIVES CANADA CATALOGUING IN PUBLICATION

Nevison, James
    Had a glass : the top 100 wines for 2006 / James Nevison, Kenji Hodgson.

Includes index.
ISBN 1-55285-727-1

    1. Wine and wine making. I. Hodgson, Kenji II. Title.

TP548.N49 2005   641.2'2   C2005-903035-6

The publisher acknowledges the financial support of the Government of Canada through the
Book Publishing Industry Development Program for our publishing activities.

contents

preface

In writing our first book, *Have a Glass: A Modern Guide to Wine*, we believed there was a need for an accessible, casual look into the world of wine. We wanted people to share our enthusiasm for keeping the good life simple. Provide the basics of wine enjoyment without the fuss, we reasoned, and the world would be a better place.

The success of *Have a Glass* was completely gratifying. The book now a national bestseller, we tip our glasses to everyone who's supported our wine writing and vinous cause.

Following *Have a Glass*, the question we were asked over and over was, "Now that I know how to drink wine, what wine should I drink?"

The follow-up, *Had a Glass*, which you're holding right now, is the answer.

Had a Glass is the companion piece to *Have a Glass*. The first book provided the information to get into wine; this book offers 100 wines worth getting into.

Sip on.

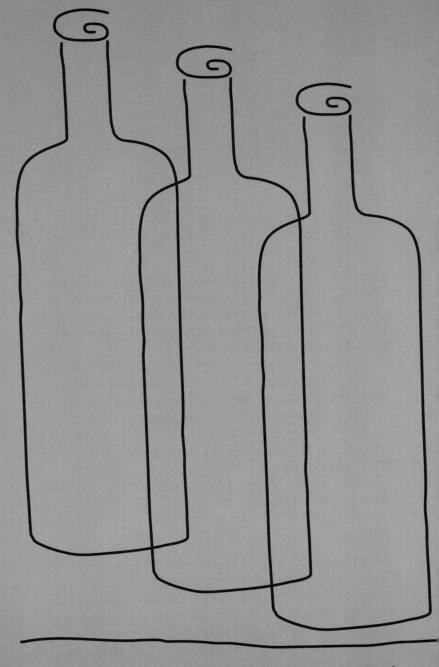

a brief guide to
wine enjoyment

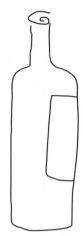

Had a Glass gives you the wine goods. In a veritable sea of vinous choice, *Had a Glass* points you in the right direction and makes sure you surface with a good bottle. And it won't cost you big money—all the wines in this book check in at under a twenty.

Each wine is here for a reason, whether it's perfect with a steak, ideal for a picnic, or simply a stand-alone sipper. And each one is a wine that we like to buy and drink.

The wines come from a swath of countries and are made of a mix of grape varieties. They're reds and whites, sweets and dries. It's wine diversity that we think you'll enjoy.

Pick a page, read the blurb, get the wine, and see what you think. Repeat often.

The Juice

We swirled and sipped through 562 different bottles to bring you the best 100. Batting a mere 0.178 means that when picking wines blindfolded—which is what wine buying is often like—only one in five wines are hits. Scary, so pack *Had a Glass* along to improve your average.

And through the gruelling work of tasting all these wines we came across a few trends. Spain is putting out some great juice at great prices. Great value from South

Know Your Liver Quaffing the grape juice is tons of fun but make sure you wine in moderation. Know your limit and always have a designated driver.

Africa, too. BC wines are showing well, and over the years we've been tasting them, there's no doubt that their calibre is rising. Globally, wine quality is at an all-time high—it's a great time to be a wine drinker.

Grape-wise, look for solid showing from Riesling and Gewürztraminer, Malbec, and Syrah. As well, the Old World is updating its look, with more bottles from France, Spain, and Italy sporting grape varieties, rather than regions, across their fronts.

The enclosure debate rages on. Other than natural cork, alternate ways to keep wine in the bottle are popping up. We twisted 19 percent screwcaps and pulled 12 percent plastic plugs. And one crown cap.

Buyer Beware

In compiling this listing, we have taken care to select wines that are widely available. We all deserve good wine, no matter where we are.

Every effort has been made to ensure prices and vintages were correct at the time of publication. That said, the vagaries of wine buying and copy deadlines conspire against us. The good buys sell out and the hot wines are subject to price increases.

Use this book as a starting point for your wine-buying adventures. Great bottles are out there, and like all good hunts, the fun is in the search.

The Value Proposition

"Value" is a dirty word, and its utterance leads to trouble. Like scoring wine on a 100-point scale, it's objective scaffolding trying to prop up a subjective framework. "Value" is at best squishy and hard to pin down. But whether you're after price rollbacks at Wal-Mart or one-of-a-kind designer pieces, true value occurs when returns exceed expectations.

Here's how value is applied in *Had a Glass*

Our bank accounts set the upper limit of our wine budget at $20. Sure, on occasion we may spend more, but overall we toe the twenty line. From our research, most of you feel the same. We all love getting a great $15 bottle of wine. But we love cracking into a tasty $10 bottle even more.

Had a Glass celebrates those wines that give you the best bottle for the buck: the $10 wines that seem like $15, the $15 bottles that stand out, the $20 wines that taste like more.

There are great wine values above and beyond— they just happen to be out of our reach. We see wine as an everyday beverage—not as a luxury—an enjoyable accessory to good living.

Wine Purveyors

If, like us, your favourite pastime is wine shopping, keep in mind you'll have quite different experiences whether you're in BC or Alberta. British Columbia wine sales are regulated by a monopoly liquor board that sets minimum prices province-wide, whereas Alberta is privatized, encouraging independent retail and competitive pricing. Whether you're cross-border shopping or not, here's a list of the goods and bads in both provinces.

British Columbia

BCLDB: These are the gov't stores, some big, many small, most of them closed Sundays and holidays.

> *The Goods:* They're in your neighbourhood. You don't have much choice.

> *The Bads:* Predictable selection. Employee uniforms. Or maybe the 80s-era polyester is good, if you dig the retro thing.

Private Shops: These might take a bit of sleuthing to find, but they're out there.

> *The Goods:* Great selection. Unusual bottles. Good service and knowledgeable staff.

> *The Bads:* Occasional price mark-ups. And the awful temptation to buy more than you went for. (They do stock empty boxes for this very problem.)

VQA Stores: Vintner's Quality Alliance is Canada's quality guarantee. VQA stores sell BC VQA-approved wines.

> *The Goods:* Unparalleled selection of BC wines. Helpful staff.

> *The Bads:* Of course, they have only BC VQA wines. Not that this is necessarily a bad thing, but try other wines, too.

Cold Beer & Wine Stores: Usually attached to a pub or hotel.

> *The Goods:* Late-night service. When everyone else is closed, you can usually find a Cold Beer that's open.

> *The Bads:* The stores are compact, so selection is limited. Price mark-ups.

Alberta

Supermarkets: Here you get your tenderloin (walk out the door and into the adjoining but separate-entranced liquor store) and a bottle of Cab. Or a case of the wine, if you're feeding the whole family.

> *The Goods:* Lower prices. Big volume means leaner mark-ups means cheaper wine—something we've never complained about.

> *The Bads:* Big volume also does away with selection, focusing on the major brands and passing over the unique, individual wines.

Boutiques: The independent stores that ooze a love for the grape. Each has its own style and vibe.

The Goods: Amazing selection and passionate staff make these boutique stores the place to go for your wine-buying adventures.

The Bads: The indie nature of these stores means you won't find one in every neighbourhood. But it's so worth the drive.

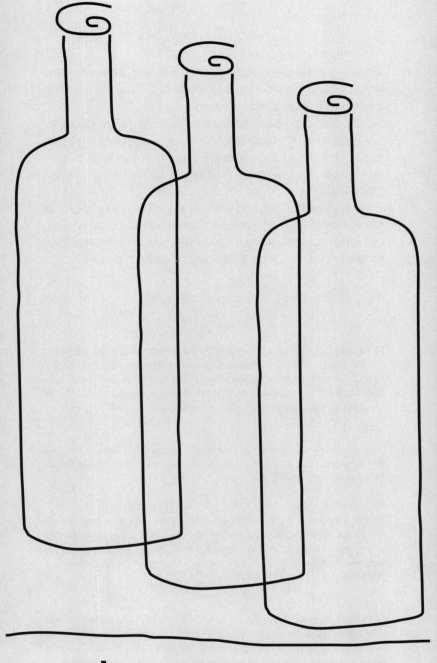

how to taste wine

Drinking wine and tasting wine are two different pastimes. If your only desire is to drink, by all means turn the page and get on to the reviews.

But if you're ready to take your wine relationship to the next level, it's time to commit to proper tasting technique. It will add to your wine enjoyment as well as permit a complete sensory evaluation of the wine in your glass, using taste, sight, smell, and feel.

We're tired of "A good wine is a wine you like." Sure, at the end of the day it's your subjective opinion that matters, but what makes a wine good? After you understand how to taste wine you'll be equipped to make that call.

Here's the wine-tasting process in four simple steps.

STEP 1 — The Look

Tilt the wineglass away from you and observe the colour against a white background. Whites can be pallid yellow to deep gold, and reds range from the rich crimson of velvet drapes to the neon of raspberry Kool-Aid. Young white wines may have the brilliant sheen of white gold, while older reds often have complex tones of browns superimposed on sombre claret. Whites are typically clear, nearly transparent, whereas a red may be slightly cloudy with sediment.

STEP 2 — The Swirl

Swirl the wineglass—either on the table or in the air—to draw out the aromas of a wine. Let the wine paint the sides of the glass with long smooth tears, or legs. Note that these indicate texture and viscosity, not necessarily quality.

STEP 3 — The Smell

Smelling is wine intimacy. A deep inhale will reveal what the wine's about. Don't be afraid to put your nose into the glass. A wine may have the aromas of fruit (melons, berries, cherries), of wood (vanilla or smoke), or of spice (pepper or clove). You may also get a whiff of less likely aromas, such as earth, diesel, and leather. Surprising maybe, but this is what makes wine exciting.

STEP 4 — The Taste

Take a mouthful of wine. Swirl it in your mouth. The consistency may be thin like skim milk (light-bodied) or it may be thick like cream (full-bodied). Let your tongue taste the different elements of the wine: any sweetness from residual sugars, any tartness from acid, or any bitterness from alcohol. Tannins may dry your gums, making you pucker. Spitting is optional.

Flights of Fancy

Becoming a good wine taster is all about tasting wines. The more wines you try, the better your frame of reference. A great way to build your database and bolster your tasting skills is to approach wine in "flights." Create a flight by lining up a few wines that share a common theme. Tasting these side by side is like taking three pairs of jeans into the changing room.

Here are a few wine flights to get you started.

Flight 1—Stylish Chardonnay

A Chardonnay is not a Chardonnay is not a Chardonnay. Wines made from the same grape can taste totally different. Try these three Chards and notice the presence—or absence—of oak (vanilla, butterscotch, toasted wood).

- A: Goundrey "Homestead Unwooded" (page 49)
- B: Michel Laroche (page 68)
- C: McWilliam's "Hanwood Estate" (page 62)

Flight 2—Syrah vs. Shiraz

Yes, they are the same grape. But the differing nomenclature can tip you off to wine style. In Oz (Australia) it's Shiraz, in France it's Syrah, and the rest of the world swaps between the two, depending on the style of the wine. Shiraz is often bold with its fruit flavours, while Syrah is typically tighter-lipped.

- A: De Bortoli "DB" Shiraz (page 90)
- B: Porcupine Ridge Syrah (page 121)
- C: Bonny Doon "Domaine des Blagueurs" Syrah-Sirrah (page 127)

Aroma vs. Bouquet To get technical, a wine's aroma is the smell derived solely from the grapes; the bouquet is that which comes from other influences, such as oak barrels and age. Aromas are the blackberries and sugar plums; bouquet is the toasted wood and brioche.

Flight 3—The case for blends

You wouldn't cook a meal from only one ingredient, so why expect a wine to be made from only one type of grape? When done right, blended wines meld the strong points of each grape variety into one synergetic potable.

A: Le Bombarde Cannonau di Sardegna (page 107) +

B: Delicato Shiraz (page 99) =

C: Chapoutier "Bila Haut." A blend of Syrah, Grenache, and Carignan (page 114)

Self-Help for Wine Monotony

If your wining has been monotonous of late, try these wine-buying strategies and never be stuck on the same bottle again.

Trust a winery

More often than not, a winery will have a particular style of winemaking, so if you like their Cabernet, chances are you'll also enjoy their Merlot, their Shiraz, or their Chardonnay. Get to know a favourite winery's whole portfolio.

If you thought the Fairview "Goats do Roam" white (page 60) was good, try their red of the same name.

Branching out

If you've been seduced by that special grape—maybe Grenache or Viognier, two very seductive cultivars—then we'd wager you'll be just as taken with the same variety made elsewhere. No infidelity here, just wine diversity.

Gewürztraminer fans are die-hard. They like their Gewürz and they're not afraid to shake it. If you like the homegrown Mt. Boucherie Gewürz (page 56) then we think you'd have an equally good time with the Pfaffenheim (page 73).

Love of the land

Certain parts of the world make certain types of wine. This is often denoted on the bottle by the appellation, or where the wine originated. Names like "Côtes du Rhône" and "Chianti" are examples. If you like the wine of a particular app, try others from the same locale.

Both the Barone Ricasoli (page 123) and the Monte Antico (page 116) hail from Tuscany in Italy, where the Sangiovese grape reigns supreme.

Trading up

A winery commonly makes different tiers of wines—the Toyota and the Lexus. *Had a Glass* is all about the Toyotas, but if you like what you're test driving, look for the luxury version.

Not many wineries can make Viognier like Yalumba in Australia. We do their "Y Series" (page 72), and if you're happy about that, take a spin with their "Eden Valley" Viognier, which breaks our budget but is worth a splurge.

Storing and Aging Your Wine

We don't mean to come across like we're down on wine cellars—quite the opposite. There's nothing we like better than rummaging around dusty wine racks sticky with cobwebs. But there's wine for aging and there's wine for drinking, and this book is about the latter.

In fact, over 90 percent of the wine sold today is made for drinking now, and to drink a wine now, you don't need a cellar. Display your wine in that IKEA wine rack, stash it in the cupboard, or keep it handy under your bed.

Mixed half-case

There's a handful of wines in this book that you could have fun with by letting them age for a few years. Put them in a box, put the box on its side, and hide it in a closet.

- Divinum Riesling Kabinett (page 64)
- Peter Lehmann Semillon (page 70)
- Quinta do Crasto Douro (page 126)
- Castillo de Molina "Reserve" Cabernet Sauvignon (page 120)
- Tinhorn Creek Cabernet Franc (page 113)
- Beyerskloof Pinotage (page 117)

Glasses and Stemware

All wineglasses aren't created equal, though drinking wine from any glass can be equally enjoyable. Allow us to explain.

Wine is like golf. There's an infinite array of specialized accessories, but all you really need to play the game is a set of clubs. Likewise, all your wine requires is a glass. It's up to you to decide how much you want to invest and how involved you want to get. Just don't tell us you can't drink wine because you don't have a glass.

There are benefits to good stemware.

- Swirling wine in the larger bowl common to high-end glasses does wonders for a wine's aromas, particularly the reds, which is why red wineglasses are larger than those for whites. Pouring a few fingers at a time lets you get a proper swirl going.

- Holding the stem helps to keep white wines chilled and grubby fingerprints off the glass.

- There's no denying the elegant tactile sensation of a thin rim caressing the lips.

We use a motley collection of crystal we've collected over the years as well as a cupboard full of everyday tumblers for backyard bashes.

Decanters

After glasses, the next most important wine accessory is the decanter. A secret to wine enjoyment, the decanter can do more for your wines than you'd imagine. Decanting old wines to remove the liquid from the sediment will keep your teeth clean, but how many of us drink old wines these days?

Use your decanter to decant young wines, letting them breathe. The vast majority of wines we buy are made to be drunk young—often too young—and decanting will open these wines up, revealing their character. Your decanter is a wine time machine, so shake and swirl with abandon.

Anything can be used as a decanter, from a clean teapot to a water jug. To get serious about your decanter, look for a glass container with a wide base and a narrow opening. This facilitates swirling, makes for easier pouring, and looks pretty sexy.

Wine Handling

Serving temperatures

18°C (65°F) a bit below room temperature	Red wine
10°C (50°F) 20 minutes out of the fridge	White (and rosé) wine
5°C (40°F) straight from the fridge	Sparkling and sweet wine

Tips

- Err on the side of serving a wine too cold. The bottle will always warm up as it sits on the table.

- If you're not enjoying the taste of a wine, chill it well and this will mask many off-flavours.

- If a wine is too sweet, serving it cold will make it taste drier.

- All dessert wine should be served at fridge temperature, unless it's red—like port—in which case serve at the same temperature as red wine.

Leftovers

Once a bottle is opened, how long do you have to drink it? It's true that wine starts to deteriorate once it's exposed to oxygen, but finishing a bottle the following day—or if you must, even the day after—is fine.

Anything past 48 hours is pushing it; you're better off breaking out a hunk of cheese and polishing off the contents before the wine starts to taste like a pumpkin.

Cork etiquette

There's no need to replace the cork after every glass is poured. Open the bottle, drink, and if there's any wine left over, put the cork back and stick it in the fridge (even reds). The cooler fridge temperature will slow down the wine's oxidization. The next day, remove reds from the fridge in time to let them warm up before serving (about one hour).

Hangover Hurt

So you imbibed a little too enthusiastically the night before and on top of an aching back from sleeping on the kitchen floor, your brain feels like it's wedged in a vice. Knock that fat head with a tried and true solution.

First things first: bust out the fluid triumvirate. Water's obvious, or if you can stagger to the corner store, then Gatorade. Beside this, place a bottle of beer. We've been known to have a beer now and again, and this is one of those occasions. Who knows why, but a lager works wonders. A Sunday Caesar will also do. The third member is comfort soup. Chicken is classic, but we say take it to the next level with a bowl of miso soup.

Work your way through these in an alternating manner while some easy-listening soothes your ringing eardrums. Something benign like Moby or some well-tempered Sade is a start. Miles or Monk if you have the jazz lying around.

If there's an ocean nearby, go jump in it. If there's a sauna, sweat it out. Bury a wineglass, beg forgiveness from Bacchus, and keep the fluids flowing.

Required Reading: Decoding a Wine Label

Wine or winery name

Back in the day, the name would be that of a chateau or domaine, or possibly it'd be a proprietary name used by a winemaking co-operative. While these are still out there, now brand names, animal species, and hip monikers are gracing wine bottles—all in an effort to help you remember what you drank.

Vintage

The year printed on the label is the year the grapes were grown. There are good years and bad years, usually determined by weather conditions.

Should you care?

In good grape-weather years there'll be more good wine, but off-years don't necessarily mean bad wine. If winemakers know what they're doing, their wines will overcome the less-than-perfect vintages. A vintage also tells you how old the wine is. Oldies aren't necessarily goodies, but many wines will improve with cellar time (see page 19).

We include the vintages for the wines we review. Where none is listed, the wine is "non-vintage," meaning it's been made from a mix of years.

Alcohol

Generally expressed as "alcohol by volume"—or ABV— this tells you how much wine you can taste before the line between "tasting" and "drinking" becomes blurred. Or blurry. As a rough guide, a higher alcohol content (14 percent is high, anything above 14.5 percent is really high) suggests a heftier, more intense wine. On the other end of the ABV spectrum, wines with less than 11 percent will often be off-dry (slightly sweet), with natural sugars.

Appellation

Or, where the grapes came from. Old world wine, say from France, often gives you the appellation instead of the grape variety. You'll see something like "Bordeaux," which describes where the grapes originated, but because French laws state only certain grapes are authorized in certain areas, the appellation name also hints at what grapes made the wine.

Grape variety

You pick up a can of soup and it's "mushroom" or "tomato." On a wine bottle it's the grape variety that defines the wine: Shiraz or Merlot or Chardonnay, to mention a few. These are your "single varietal" wines, as opposed to "blended" wines, the likes of Cabernet-Merlot and Semillon -Sauvignon Blanc. Keep in mind, single varietal wines are no better than blends and vice versa. It all comes down to good winemaking creating good-tasting wine. Trust your taste buds.

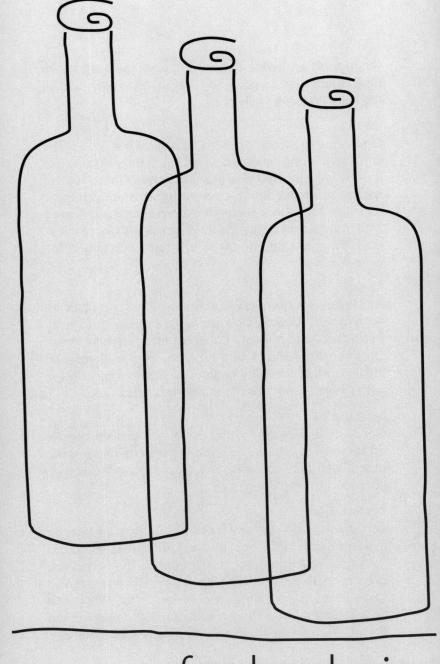

food and wine

When food and wine harmonize, your meal moves to new heights. It's an epiphany we can all experience—if the wine gods are smiling.

Intensity

Big-flavoured wines go with big-flavoured foods. The corollary is light-flavoured wines suit lighter dishes. This is a key reason why a hearty Shiraz doesn't fit well with a garden salad, but damn, it's amazing with lamb chops.

Think, too, about the wine's alcohol content. A wine with more alcohol usually comes across with more intensity. This might tip you off as to what kind of food the wine will match.

Flavour

Food and wine flavours will either match or contrast with each other. A buttery Chardonnay matches a creamy alfredo pasta and a meaty Cabernet matches, well, meat. On the other hand, a racy, crisp Sauvignon Blanc is an ideal contrast for briny oysters, and salty blue cheese with sweet dessert wine is a famous combo.

Tweak Your food

Got an extra peppery Shiraz? Grind a bit of black pepper on the dish to bridge the gap. Is that zesty Riesling too overpowering? Squeeze a few drops of lemon juice on your food to help things jive.

Balance Your food

Can any wine go with any food? If your food is balanced in flavour, your chances of a successful match will triple.

A steak or a salmon on its own can be too humdrum, but a sprinkle of salt and a bit of lemon will give the dish some balance. And if you counter an acidic vinaigrette on a garden salad with a handful of roasted pine nuts or bacon bits, you'll increase your wine-pairing success rate.

Icons

These icons will reappear in our list of top wines.

Food Icons

Wine and food together is gastronomy in stereo. To help your pairings sing, here are some general guidelines.

BEEF
Big protein:
roast, steak, stew.

CHEESE
Hard or soft,
stinky or mild.

CHOCOLATE
The darker
the better.

FISH
Trout, salmon,
halibut, tuna.

ON ITS OWN

PORK
The other white meat!
Chops, kebabs, tenderloin.

POULTRY
Turkey, chicken,
duck, guinea fowl.

SHELLFISH
Bi-valves, oh my!
Oysters, mussels, clams.

SPICY
Szechuan,
mild curry, Thai.

VEGETARIAN
Tofu-friendly: stir-fries,
ratatouille, mushrooms galore.

Occasion Icons

Wine is tied to experience. There's a wine for every occasion, but certain times call for specific wines. Whether the moment is casual or formal, serious or celebratory, a glass of wine can match the mood.

APERITIF
Suitable pre-meal to get the
gastro-juices flowing.

BEGINNER
Easy to drink, varietally
true wines.

BYO
Crowd-pleasers; wines
to pack along.

CELLAR
Wines that get better
after a couple of years.

PATIO/PICNIC
Hot weather sipping wines.

ROCK OUT
Wines to let your hair down, tussle that doo, and coif that mullet.

ROMANCE
Wines to get busy with.

WEDNESDAY WINE
To get you through the mid-week hump.

WINE GEEK
Wines on the esoteric side that only a geek could love.

WINTER WARMER
Wines to ward off any chill.

A glass of wine a day? Riedel's Sommelier Series Bordeaux glass holds an entire bottle of wine!

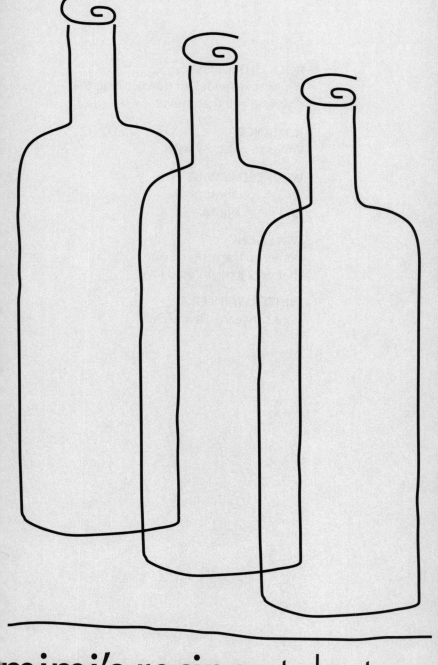

mimi's recipes take two

Mimi gave us a handful of delicious recipes for our first book, *Have a Glass: A Modern Guide to Wine*. Telling us we have to build our recipe repertoire, she's back with four wine-friendly dishes. For each recipe, we've selected three wines to pour alongside.

Chicken tastes like chicken until you stuff it! This tri-colour stuffing seduces both the taste buds and the eyeballs.

bacchus stuffed chicken

prep time 15 minutes | **cooking time** 35 minutes | **makes** 4 servings

2 handfuls	spinach
¼ cup (50 mL)	feta cheese, crumbled
4	sun-dried tomatoes, finely sliced
2 Tbsp (30 mL)	pine nuts
4	large chicken thighs, skin on
¼ cup (50 mL)	vegetable oil or olive oil
to taste	salt and pepper

1　Preheat oven to 350°F (180°C).
2　Wilt spinach in a hot, dry pan.
3　Combine spinach, cheese, tomato, and pine nuts.
4　Carefully stuff mixture between skin and meat of thighs.
5　Heat oil over medium-high heat in ovenproof skillet. Add thighs skin-side down and brown for 5 minutes, then brown other side for 5 minutes. Season with salt and pepper.
6　Place chicken in oven and bake until meat is cooked through, about 25 minutes.

note *For a sauce/gravy, deglaze pan with white wine.*

serve 1. **Lorch Riesling (page 53), 2. Cellier de Marrenon Rosé (page 77), 3. Nk'Mip Cellars Pinot Noir (page 118)**

Legend has it that this pasta is named after the "working ladies" who needed an easy fix after an evening's work. They sure could cook.

quick and easy pasta puttanesca

prep time 15 minutes | **cooking time** 15 minutes | **makes** 4 servings

4 Tbsp (50 mL)	olive oil
½ cup (125 mL)	onions, chopped
2 Tbsp (30 mL)	capers, chopped
¼ cup (50 mL)	black olives (kalamata), sliced
2 Tbsp (30 mL)	garlic, chopped
4 tsp (20 mL)	anchovies, well drained and chopped
	(omit for a vegetarian version)
2 cups (500 mL)	cherry tomatoes, halved
large handful	fresh basil, chopped (or 2 tsp./10 mL dried basil)
¼ cup (50 mL)	fresh Italian parsley, chopped
to taste	chili flakes
generous pinch	salt (more if anchovies are omitted)
12 oz (350 g)	dried pasta
to taste	freshly grated Parmesan cheese

1 Heat heavy-bottomed saucepan over medium heat. Add olive oil and pinch of salt.
2 Add onions and cook until softened but not brown.
3 Add capers, olives, garlic, and anchovies, and simmer for 1 minute.
4 Add cherry tomatoes, basil, parsley, and chili flakes, and simmer for 5 minutes.
5 Cook pasta.
6 Drain pasta, reserving ½ cup (125 mL) pasta water. Toss pasta, water, and sauce together.
7 Top with freshly grated parmesan just before serving.

serve 1. Marqués de Riscal Rueda (page 69), 2. Mateus Rosé (page 76), 3. Di Majo Norante Sangiovese (page 108)

At Mimi's homestead the cycle of life is complete. Last year we helped herd this lamb, now it's on our plate. And damn, it's tasty.

mimi's braised lamb

prep time 15 minutes | **cooking time** 2½ hours | **makes** 4 servings

3 Tbsp (45 mL)	olive oil
2.2 lb (1 kg)	lamb leg, bone-in
1½	onions, sliced
3	carrots, sliced
2 Tbsp (30 mL)	garlic, chopped
4 small sprigs	fresh rosemary
1 tsp (5 mL)	sea salt
¼ tsp (1 mL)	freshly ground black pepper
1 cup (250 mL)	red wine
½ cup (125 mL)	lamb stock (or water)

1 Heat 1½ Tbsp (22 mL) of olive oil in a heavy-bottomed saucepan over medium-high heat. Brown the lamb on all sides and remove it from the pot.

2 Heat remaining olive oil in the same saucepan. Add onions, carrots, and garlic. Cook the vegetables on medium-low heat for 15 minutes until caramelized.

3 Return lamb to saucepan. Add rosemary, salt, pepper, wine, and stock. Cover and braise (simmer) on low heat until tender, about 2½ hours.

4 Remove lamb to a heated platter and remove rosemary sprigs from braising liquid.

5 Place vegetables and liquid into blender and purée.

6 Slice lamb and serve with the gravy.

note *If there's any gravy left over, save it and use it as a base for a soup.*

serve 1. **Mad Dogs & Englishmen Monastrell-Shiraz-Cabernet Sauvignon** (page 110), 2. **Veramonte Merlot** (page 104), 3. **Columbia Crest "Two Vines" Shiraz** (page 122)

Before drive-thrus and home delivery there was gratin, which in one fell swoop (and in one pot) satisfies all cravings for carbs, protein, and vegetables.

retro comfort gratin

prep time 30 minutes | **cooking time** 30 minutes | **makes** 4 servings

4	medium potatoes, sliced 1/2 inch (1.2 cm) thick
2 lb (0.9 kg)	raw sausage (e.g., Toulouse or Coq au Vin), cut into 1-inch (2.5-cm) slices
2 Tbsp (30 mL)	butter (or olive oil)
2	medium leeks, including green stalks, washed well and sliced
1	large clove garlic, minced
½	head cabbage, thinly sliced
pinch	salt
½ tsp (3 mL)	freshly ground black pepper
2 Tbsp (30 mL)	vegetable oil

1 Place the potatoes in a pot of cold, salted water. Bring to a boil and simmer for 5 minutes or until just tender. Drain, remembering to save the vegetable water for soup or gravy.

2 In an ovenproof pot or saucepan, brown the sausage over medium heat. Remove and set aside.

3 In the same pot, heat the butter or olive oil and add the leeks, garlic, and cabbage. Season with salt and pepper to taste and cook, covered, over low heat for 15 minutes or until the cabbage is wilted and tender.

4 Preheat oven to 400°F (200°C).

5 Spread potato and sausage slices evenly over cabbage and leek mix. Drizzle with vegetable oil and bake for 15 minutes. Crank the oven to broil for 10 minutes or until the potatoes are golden.

**serve 1. Dunavar "Connoisseur Collection" Pinot Gris (page 36),
2. Lujuria (page 80), 3. La Bastide (page 84)**

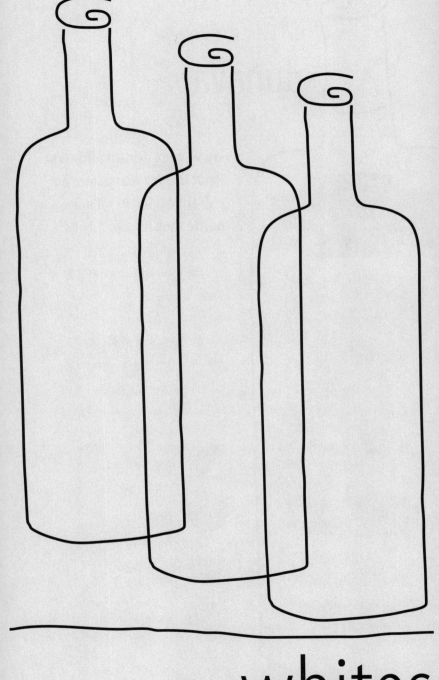

the whites

dunavar

We've been drinking Dunavar Pinot Gris for years, since an old lady tipped us off in a bottle shop lineup. Though the price has crept up a bit, it still offers amazing value. And we maintain a brazen sense of satisfaction from drinking a "Connoisseur Collection" wine for under a tenner. This Pinot Gris is straight-up and honest, offering scents of apple blossoms and peaches. It's a perennial go-to white.

 pan-fried cod

 cheddar

 on its own

 Wednesday

**2003 | Pinot Gris
"Connoisseur Collection"
Hungary
$8.99**

blue nun

Wine wankers love to talk about their "eureka" moment.

This means the moment when they realized they love wine, usually accompanied by a serious ego stroke. We don't do eureka moments but we will say this: a buddy of ours once poured for us a series of white German wines without telling us what they were. We chose our favourite and when the dust settled, whaddya know, it was Blue Nun.

 braised chicken

 ribs

 on its own

 Wednesday, aperitif

**2003
Germany
$9.95**

viña tarapaca

Sauvignon Blanc should always be this cheap. It's such the love-me wine with its fresh and clean disposition, and in our Anne-of-Green-Gables world everyone would be able to get with SB. We can't ever remember a time when some joker came up to us asking for a $100 Sauvignon Blanc. The Tarapaca is what real people want to drink, and $10 is what real people want to spend.

basa kebabs

steamed prawns

stir-fry

patio/picnic, beginner

**2004
Sauvignon Blanc
Chile
$9.99**

domaine de sancet

Here's your "house white" of distinction—the Sancet will do you right on most occasions.
And at this price you can afford to keep a few in the fridge. With a hint of sweetness in this wine's finish, we do suggest you serve it well-chilled to keep things fresh. Look for lively lemon, lime, and honeysuckle with a splash of pink grapefruit. Supple and well-balanced, it's an example of the potential—and value—from backwoods France.

 broiled mackerel

 mapo tofu

 BYO, aperitif

2004
Vin de Pays des
Côtes du Gascogne
France
$9.99

gazela

Vinho verde is Portuguese for green wine, and even your city-slicking grasp of grapes should tip you off that the fruit is picked just underripe and the resulting wine is bottled young. It's like soda pop for grown-ups: cheap, extremely refreshing, and with a slight petulance that dances across the tongue. Vinho Verde's tame alcoholic strength and zippy nature makes it the perfect patio sipper.

 curry

 on its own

 patio/picnic, rock out

**2004
Vinho Verde
Portugal
$9.99**

It takes about 500 grapes to make a bottle of wine.

hardys

Hardys' RG is perfect for "getting into wine." It's also perfect for "getting out of wine." If there's trepidation around plunging into some potent red wines and you want a friendlier edge, here's your vino. Or, if all you've been drinking are monster reds and you need an off-dry fix, this is also your wine. Super-aromatic with gummy bears and honey, it's hard not to be wooed. Yes, it's sweet, and yes, it's easygoing, but chill this puppy as cold as you can, serve lots of it in large tumblers, and your palate will thank us.

 on its own

 beginner

**2004
Riesling-Gewürztraminer
Australia
$9.99**

cono sur

Time and time again this wine has wowed us. It's consistent through vintages, and with a plastic cork, you can be sure you'll get all the freshness that Viognier promises. Next year we hope they'll do screwcap, but for the time being the plastic plug works well. True to its cultivar origins, the Cono Sur has generous aromas of ripe peaches, apricots, honeysuckle, and a slice of ginger root. It's a well-balanced drop with a pleasantly lingering aftertaste. Solid wine, solid value.

**2004
Viognier
Chile
$10.99**

 pan-fried scallops

 Szechuan

 winter warmer, BYO

lurton

Pinot Gris comes in so many styles, but here's one that stays true to the grape—and one that won't dent your pocketbook. But what's true Gris? Many of the best come with a captivating, fragrant, even soapy aroma, along with just the slightest whiff of cheese. It's honest varietal character, and when combined with its other ripe peach, honeydew, and tropical fruit qualities, it's perfect. The Lurton demos this with great balance and soft, yet concentrated flavours. Great Gris at a great price.

 Cornish game hen

 pan-fried trout

 Brie

 patio/picnic, romance

2004
Pinot Gris
Argentina
$10.99

lindemans

Trying to think of a better-value Aussie Riesling than the Bin 75, we come up dry. This wine is the definition of bottled freshness, with racy lemon and lime citrus flavours and a super-crisp finish, preserved in a perfect state by the screwcap closure. If you're not sure about Riesling, note that this one has no cloying sweetness. Chill and serve alongside Chinese or Thai takeout; with no cork to screw things up, you get good wine, all the time.

 salad

 sautéed shrimp

 Chinese or Thai

 patio/picnic

**2004
Riesling "Bin 75"
Australia
$11.49**

lurton

Many top Sauvignon Blancs are prized for their pungent, almost smoky aromas that bring to mind flint or stones, particularly true of the wines from France's famed Pouilly-Fumé region. At $12, Les Fumées Blanches is Pouilly-lite, and a great introduction to this classic Sauv Blanc style. Grapefruit and fresh-cut grass segue into the rich suppleness, not to mention the hint of flint and chalk, that grounds this good-value white. (To really gauge the wine's smokiness, let it breathe in the glass for some time.)

 raw oysters

 broiled asparagus

 wine geek, BYO

**2003
Sauvignon Blanc
"Les Fumées Blanches"
France
$11.99**

2004
Riesling "Classic Dry"
British Columbia
$12.49

gehringer brothers

We like our shirts untucked and our shoes sans laces. That said, this laissez-faire fashion sense has its limitations. Sometimes it's nice to slip on the button-down and spit-shine the two-tones. In these moments of reserve, we opt for appropriately austere wines. Classy, much like Gehringer whites. The Gehringer Brothers are meticulous in their wine craftsmanship, and the Classic Dry is all about peach skin, faint mineral, and a deft, light touch. Sniff, sip, swallow. Repeat. It's easy to get along with; the well-manicured, less intrusive wines always end up being the best dining companions.

baked sole

 steamed clams

 Wednesday, beginner

lang

Riesling's the Mini Disc of wine. Great idea and lots going for it, but people were slow to catch on and the hype fizzled. Now everyone's drinking Sauvignon Blanc and listening to their iPod. But hot or not, the Valley grows some good Riesling, and Lang gives you tasty wine at affordable prices. Soft aromas of white peach and Spartan apples segue to lemon candy and sticky honey flavours. There's a streak of sweetness that's balanced nicely by a tangy finish.

 roast pork

 turkey sandwich

 tacos

 Wednesday, BYO

LANG
VINEYARDS

2004
Farm Winery Reserve
Riesling
VQA • OKANAGAN VALLEY • VQA
WHITE WINE • VIN BLANC

**2004
Riesling
"Farm Reserve"
British Columbia
$12.90**

the little penguin

**2003
Chardonnay
Australia
$12.99**

With all these animal labels now on wine bottles, the liquor store's a regular Noah's Ark. The Little Penguin waddles its way to the tabletop. There's a richness here that belies the wine's price tag. A nose full of apple pie and meringue leads to ripe apple flavours and a nice clove spiciness. Call it an "amply-oaked" Chardonnay, but the wood helps create a robust, viscous wine that sticks with you.

 grilled chicken

 on its own

 winter warmer, beginner

goundrey

Oaked vs. unoaked? For Chardonnay, that's the question. We wish it weren't so black or white—it's not like you can like only acoustic or electric guitar. There's no denying the richness that emanates from a well-crafted wooden guitar body, and you can't fault technology's ability to massage pure, clean sound. The Goundrey Unwooded Chard is plugged in to refreshment, brimming with apple and honeydew. Definitely the Fender of Chardonnays.

 deep fried tofu

 sautéed swordfish

 patio/picnic, Wednesday

2004
Chardonnay
"Homestead Unwooded"
Australia
$12.99

Jars of wine in King Tutankhamun's tomb (d. 1352 BC) had labels with enough detail to satisfy Australian labelling laws, except that they didn't reveal the grape varieties.

inniskillin

2004
**Pinot Blanc
"Reserve"
British Columbia**
$12.99

Pinot Blanc suffers from Hollywood chick-flick syndrome: mostly unmemorable.

Traditionally derided as "poor man's Chardonnay" (which seems outdated to us given the pools of cheap Chardonnay out there), most Pinot Blancs will pass off as mere bit players to another meal. Not this bottle. The Inniskillin Pinot Blanc is PB in a three-piece—classy—offering rich apple and canned pineapple flavours. It's plump, juicy, has a nice balance, and is refreshing both in flavour and originality.

 pork chops

 baked yam

 seared tuna

 romance, BYO

calona

If rappers really understood high living they'd praise "Pinot G" as the real deal, at least in the Okanagan, where the grape continues to make a mark for itself. Calona's "Artist Series" Pinot Gris is a consistent performer. It offers up bright apple and citrus, a soft mouth feel, and a crisp finish in a package that's remarkable in its modesty. Like the sixth wine off the bench, you can count on this bottle to anchor a meal.

 curry

 on its own

 Wednesday, beginner

**2004
Pinot Gris
"Artist Series"
British Columbia
$12.99**

rh phillips

**2003
Chardonnay
California
$12.99**

The big news on this bottle is its bright orange enclosure, a proprietary screwcap that's svelte, fun to touch, and looks like something off a 2-6-er of vodka. But we like to think we're mature enough not to be seduced by a pretty face; it's what's inside that counts—a lively Chardonnay showing apple and creamy vanilla aromas that build to citrusy, lemon-rind flavours, and a refreshing finish. Easygoing and easy to open!

 Schnitzel

 beercan chicken

 picnic, BYO

lorch

No syrupy German Riesling here! The Lorch derives from Pfalz, the area in Germany known for gutsy, vehement white wines. Pfalz kicks out drier, even fiery, Rieslings, and Lorch delivers this in spades. A whiff reveals citrus and slate aromas, followed by flavours of green apples and honey. You might need to pour an extra glass as you get used to this austere style—this is wine geek wine, but the Lorch speaks to those who like a drier Riesling.

 pulled pork

 Thanksgiving turkey

 wine geek

Weingut Lorch

2003
RIESLING
HOCHGEWÄCHS
BERGZABERNER ALTENBERG
PFALZ
750 ml
GUTSABFÜLLUNG

**2003
Riesling
Germany
$12.99**

torres

TORRES

Viña Esmeralda

MOSCATEL - GEWÜRZTRAMINER

VIN BLANC SEMI-SEC - SEMI-DRY WHITE WINE

EMBOUTEILLÉ PAR - BOTTLED BY
MIGUEL TORRES, S.A. - 08720 - BARCELONA - ESPAÑA
PRODUIT D'ESPAGNE - PRODUCT OF SPAIN

11% alc./vol. 750 mL

**2004
Moscatel-Gewürztraminer
"Viña Esmeralda"
Spain
$13.99**

Here's aromatherapy that we can get into. Nothing comforts like the scents wafting from a glass full of Viña Esmeralda. A blend of two aromatic grapes—Moscatel (Muscat) and Gewürztraminer—is responsible for the huge aromas of pear, mangoes, and blooming flowers in this olfactory juggernaut.

 broiled catfish

 steamed mussels

 Thai noodles

 romance, aperitif

bonnet-huteau

Wine is about occasion. A wine might taste like crap when you're at some lousy party eating stale soda crackers and listening to a freakshow talk about his ailing komodo dragon. Then the same wine might make you kneel and praise Bacchus when you taste it on a deliciously lazy Saturday afternoon while a Coltrane record spins in the background. Muscadet has time and place, and time and place have Muscadet. The Bonnet-Huteau is racy with citrus and mineral streaks, awash in refreshment value.

 baked skate

 oyster poorboy

 picnic

2003
Muscadet Sur Lie
France
$14.25

mt. boucherie

**2003
Gewürztraminer
British Columbia
$14.40**

Sleeper Gewürz! BC has been able to do Germanic grape varieties ever since it's had latitudinal similarities, but here's bottled proof of its fancy for Deutschland cuttings. Boucherie does a great rendition of a just-dry-enough style that keeps pace with your meal and still satisfies the sweet tooth. Classic Gewürz aromas of rose petals and lychee come off this wine along with bonus material of peach and tropical fruits. This wine shows a style worth applauding the home team for.

 lobster bisque

 curry

 Morbier

 Wednesday, BYO

fazi battaglia

Fazi sports its retro-cool bottle with panache. Ergonomically correct for repeated pouring, the glass references old Roman amphorae. Complete with paper scroll strung around its neck, the Fazi is a conversation piece for any patio table. Inside, the wine is light and crisp. Honeysuckle and blanched almond aromas highlight an old-school style. It won't be remembered for its complexity, but sometimes a wine is best when it plays a supporting—not starring—role.

 calamari

 shrimp fondue

 wine geek, aperitif

**2003
Verdicchio
Italy
$14.90**

wild goose

WILD GOOSE
V I N E Y A R D S
GEWURZTRAMINER
2004
VQA   OKANAGAN VALLEY   VQA
13.5% Alc./Vol.   White Wine Vin Blanc   750 ml
Produced by A.F. Kruger & Sons, Okanagan Falls, BC
Product of British Columbia, Canada Produit de la Columbie-Britannique, Canada

**2004
Gewürztraminer
British Columbia
$14.95**

Grapes make the wine, so if you have lousy fruit you get lousy wine. Done well, great grapes make very great wine. A synergistic meeting of vineyard location and grape variety is the key to the transcendental, like Rick Moranis and Sigourney Weaver in the first *Ghostbusters*. Wild Goose is seriously tuned into some great Gewürz in a great spot in the Valley, and they turn out a stylish lychee and grapefruit candy wine that's drier than a lot of other Gewürztraminers from BC.

 smoked ham

 jerk tofu

 patio/picnic, beginner

bertani

We actually stopped drinking sub-$20 Soave for some time out of downright disgust at the river of mediocre wine from this appellation in northeast Italy. But the pendulum's in swing and things are looking up—though don't get starry-eyed about anything Soave just yet. Look for the Classico stuff (the favourable vineyard sites) and the Superiore stuff (better grapes, matured longer) like this Bertani. Soft, peachy aromas with a splash of almonds and crushed flowers. Deliciously waxy and luscious. Soave, indeed.

 salt-cured mackerel

 crab cakes

 wine geek, romance

**2003
Soave Classico Superiore
Italy
$14.95**

fairview

**2004
"Goats do Roam"
South Africa
$14.99**

Sure, the Côtes du Rhône/ Goats do Roam joke is getting played out, but Fairview really does have a bunch of goats wandering the property. The goats have a fine time merrily climbing the goat tower, but best of all their milk makes some tasty cheese. The white GdR (there's also a red version) is rich with aromas of peaches and almonds. The wine is well-balanced with a good, weighty texture that makes it immediately likeable. Of course once you try the wine, the joke's on you because the GdR truly speaks of CdR.

 chicken satay

 salmon amandine

 Manchego

 wine geek, romantic

wynns

Aussie Riesling typically tends towards fruity, vibrant, and dry—bone dry. It becomes delectable when you get all this in a package under $15. Wynns Riesling is a wine with a mission, laser-like in its focus on utter refreshment. So crisp and zippy it'll near wipe the enamel off your teeth, this wine gushes lime zest and lemon drop flavours. True Riesling from Oz.

 baked oysters

 Korean hotpot

 rock out, cellar

**2004
Riesling
Australia
$14.99**

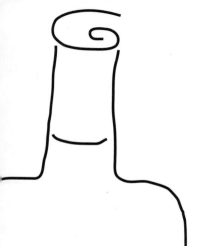

mᶜwilliam's

If *Vice* magazine printed the dos and don'ts of wine, in the latter they'd have a pic of a fashion-depraved and/or drunk oak barrel with the caption, "Someone better tell him no one likes oak anymore." Of course they'd be dead wrong and we'd have the Hanwood to prove it. What makes the difference? Balance. The oak flavours—vanilla, toast, caramel—aren't sitting out there in left field but are blended nicely into the wine. Also check the crisp acidity that fingers flabby Chardonnay.

 fried chicken

 on its own

 winter warmer, rock out

**2002
Chardonnay
"Hanwood Estate"
Australia
$14.99**

WINE TUNES: Bloc Party's "Silent Alarm"

rosemount estate

These days everyone's starting to look the same. Too much zigging and not enough zagging. With current wine fashions pushing the zippy, bracing style of Sauvignon Blanc, it's easy to overlook the grape's other, more robust side. Plump aromas of papaya and kiwi fruit dominate, and a rich, honeyed texture makes for satisfying sipping. A bright acidity freshens things up in the finish; this is tailored SB from a respected house, not wine fashion of the day.

 stuffed chicken thighs

 Gruyère

 romance, Wednesday

**2003
Sauvignon Blanc
"Diamond Label"
Australia
$15.49**

divinum

We love hock bottles. No one tries to put a huge punt on the tall and skinny bottle, perpetrating the myth that a bigger punt means a better wine. The hock bottle looks classy on the dinner table, fits nicely in your hand, and pours well. If it won't fit the door of your fridge, put it horizontal above the veggie drawer. Check the Divinum's glass curves and rub your thumb on the textured label. Drink up the slate and ozone aromas. Taste the lime and honey flavours.

 spare ribs

 salt and pepper squid

 on its own

 picnic, cellar

**2003
Riesling Kabinett
Germany
$15.50**

What the Punt? Punts are the dimples in the bottom of the wine bottle. They work to trap any sediment that's in the wine, but contrary to popular belief, they're not good for gripping and they don't reflect wine quality. Not to be confused with punters, who are heavy imbibers not concerned with punt size at all.

sandhill

Someone obviously forgot to tell winemaker Howard Soon that Pinot Blanc is a frou-frou grape. By barrel-fermenting in new American oak, Sandhill has crafted a robust, wonderfully textural wine. Redolent apple and pear tones lead to a lingering, honeyed finish. Very stylish—in a high-street kind of way—from the minimalist label to the elegant wine inside.

 roasted tenderloin

 lasagna

 winter warmer, BYO

**2003
Pinot Blanc
British Columbia
$15.99**

de wetshof

**2004
Chardonnay Sur Lie
"Danie De Wet"
South Africa
$15.99**

Wine euphemisms are nothing new. How many sugar-coated reviews cite "barnyard aromas" instead of saying "stinks like cow dung"; how many say "potent" instead of "burns like industrial-strength alcohol." So when the yeast cells check out after converting grape juice into wine, and they're left in contact with the wine to add flavour and texture, no one says the wine's been "sitting around on dregs." No, "sur lie" is the call. Revel in the soft creaminess brought to you by the lees; relish the fresh apple skin and melon flavours of this fine Chardonnay.

 fried chicken

 on its own

 winter warmer, BYO

quails' gate

The Quails' Gate Chenin is exactly what we want more of from our backyard vintners: great quality at a great price.

Not much Chenin from the Okanagan, so jump on this rarity: aromatic and fresh, with some lemon, honey, and a touch of a mineral-like complexity on the nose. But trumping all of this is the smell of grass. Not that kind of grass—this is like standing in the middle of a spring meadow, dew still drying on the clover-padded field. Lame wine metaphors aside, this wine is that vibrant, refreshing white you've been looking for.

 blackened halibut

 seafood pasta

 jerk tofu

 patio/picnic, rock out

**2004
Chenin Blanc
"Limited Release"
British Columbia
$15.99**

michel laroche

This Chard doesn't so much wow! as it seduces through quirky character, like that style-to-spare hipster girl walking on the other side of the street. What are you waiting for? Run across and explain you'd love to treat her to a postmodern Chardonnay unafraid to embrace a bit of classical barrel fermentation and mineral textures while eschewing big fruitiness.

 roasted quail

 baked lingcod

 romance, wine geek

2002
Chardonnay
France
$15.99

Wine Tunes: Serge Gainsbourg's "Comic Strip"

marqués de riscal

So many good white wines get shafted because people would rather drop cash on red. Bang for buck they think a red will deliver more. More what? So much red sells because it says "Cabernet" or "Shiraz"—it's high time we get into some serious white wines. And we're not talking sleazy Chards or copycat Sauvignon Blancs. This Rueda delivers stand-up flavour and complexity and should be pivotal in the "white is the new red" trend for 2006.

 jambalaya

 seafood paella

 picnic, BYO

2003
Rueda
Spain
$15.99

peter lehmann

**2003
Semillon
Australia
$15.99**

So the label is graced by a naked woman. The breast-baring femme might be cubist and Picasso-esque, but it was enough to get the label banned in the USA. The bottle's not pornographic, though the wine inside borders on hedonism. Young Semillon is truly a thing to behold. Currently, the Lehmann is tight and tart, flaunting amazing lime and lanolin. But give this baby a few years and it'll develop into a rich, toasty, honeyed wine. It's one of the few whites under $20 that would be at home in a cellar.

 three-bean casserole

 broiled monkfish

 periwinkles

 patio/picnic, cellar

babich

Kiwi Sauvignon Blanc is a wine for rockers. The wine's bold kick hits like a power chord straight to the palate. The Babich intros with a barrage of ripe gooseberry, grass, and asparagus; head bang to a zippy, lemon zest chorus with an herbaceous riff from start to finish. Turning down the bland and turning up the fresh, it's for those who like to rock out from time to time. Give 'er wine.

 butterflied prawns

 on its own

 romance, rock out

**2004
Sauvignon Blanc
New Zealand
$17.99**

Wine Tunes: The Jon Spencer Blues Explosion's "Extra Width"

yalumba

YALUMBA

AUSTRALIA'S OLDEST FAMILY OWNED WINERY

SOUTH AUSTRALIA
VIOGNIER
2004

THE YALUMBA WINE
COMPANY HAS CRAFTED
THIS WINE TO HIGHLIGHT
THE DIVERSITY AND
REGIONAL CHARACTER
OF SOUTH AUSTRALIA'S
RENOWNED WINE AREAS.

WHITE WINE PRODUCT OF AUSTRALIA

2004
Viognier
"Y Series"
Australia
$17.99

This bottle oozes aromas of rose petals so seductive it could double as perfume in a pinch and a supple apricot syrup texture that would work as pancake topper any time of the day. Yalumba is a Viognier specialist, and the "Y Series" captures the essence of the grape wonderfully. If ever you were looking for the perfect wine to sip from a partner's "innie," you've found it.

 nachos

 on its own

 aperitif, rock out

pfaffenheim

We searched your liquor store high and low to bring you the best Alsatian Gewürz for under $20. Okay, so this is the only Gewürztraminer from the German-esque appellation of Alsace that checks in at under twenty, but let's just be thankful that it's damn tasty. Gewürz comes in all shapes and sizes, from sticky-sweet dessert wine to dry table wine, but all good examples reveal the unmistakably aromatic character of this variety. The Pfaffenheim is a hands-down stunning find; look for a nose-full of roses and white pepper, apple skins, and poached pears.

 lentil cassoulet

 Explorateur

 wine geek, romance

**2003
Gewürztraminer
France
$18.99**

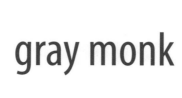

gray monk

It stands to reason that a winery named after the Pinot Gris grape would deliver a quality namesake wine. The Heiss family pretty much gave Pinot Gris a home in the Okanagan, planting their first vineyards over thirty years ago! Theirs is the oldest family-owned-and-operated winery in the Valley, and the Odyssey Pinot Gris is the culmination of their Gris efforts. A wine of remarkable richness and depth, there's more peach pit and dreamy floral notes than a puffy pop ditty. For our money, this is BC's top Pinot Gris.

**2003
Pinot Gris
"Odyssey"
British Columbia
$19.99**

 chicken Cordon Bleu

 oysters Rockefeller

 on its own

 patio/picnic, BYO

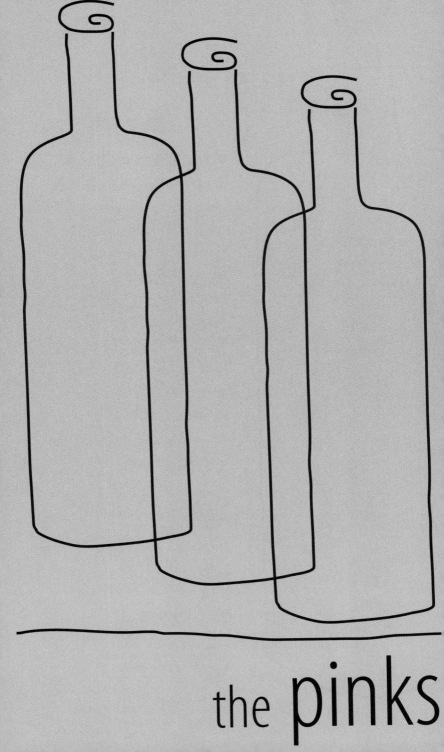

the pinks

mateus

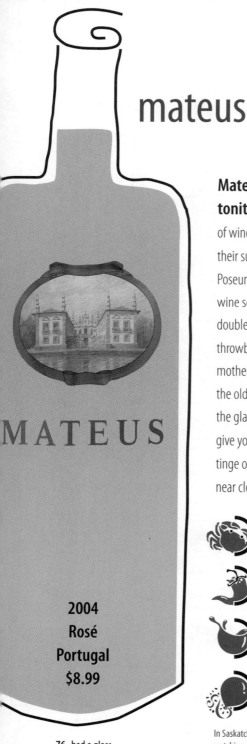

MATEUS

2004
Rosé
Portugal
$8.99

Mateus is like bottled kryptonite. Take it anywhere near a circle of wine snobs and they'll cringe and lose their super wine-sniffing superpowers. Poseurs. It's hard to think of another wine so capable of pulling double duty on the patio and at a throwback 70s party. This isn't your mother's Mateus; it's drier in style than the old incarnation. Bright fuchsia in the glass, the wine jumps right out to give you a slap and a tickle: very berry, a tinge of petulance, off-dry but nowhere near cloying. Lip-smacking.

 steamed mussels

 tacos

 on its own

 picnic, aperitif

In Saskatchewan, it's illegal to drink alcohol while watching exotic dancers.

cellier de marrenon

Don't deny it—you thought about buying a pink polo shirt last summer. And for those who took the plunge, how perfectly would a glass of salmon-hued wine, condensing in the summer swelter, reflect the hipster look? Then when you get berated for drinking sugar-coated White Zin, you chase them off with cries of "Dry! This wine is dry!" Which indeed it is, and that's why we love it. A blend of Syrah and Grenache, it's a richer style rosé with a great, spicy finish—suitable for all your BBQ and picnic needs.

 chicken cacciatore

 curry

 romance, Wednesday

**2004
Côtes du Luberon Rosé
France
$12.95**

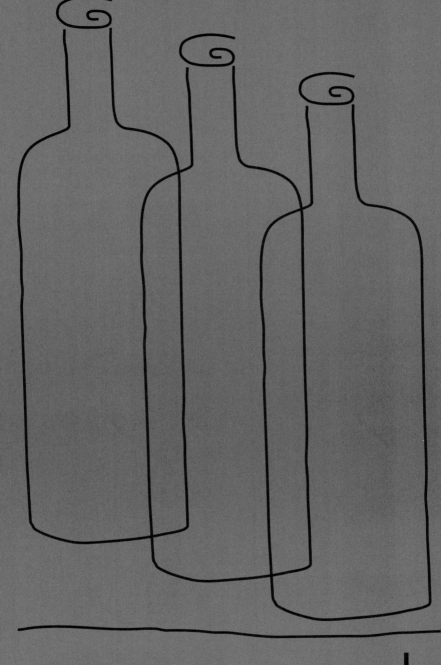

the reds

lujuria

It's all fun and nouveau-riche to run around spending big bucks on wine, but sometimes you just want to be low-brow and bohemian and get something that costs less than $10. For this, there's the Lujuria. It's a blend of Merlot and Monastrell (monastrell is Spanish, mourvèdre is French; same grape) and the wine comes from Yecla (a hot and dry region in southern Spain), but does any of this matter? The wine is under a tenner, dude. Heady aromas of smoky plums and dried herbs, ample flavours of ripe fruit. Nice wine at a nice price.

2002
Yecla
Spain
$8.95

 stew

 cheese

 winter warmer, Wednesday

fossi

Without fail, every time we brown-bag this at a tasting for wine industry types, it comes out near the top. Everyone's busy nosing all the fancy Bordeaux and Riojas, but when we tally the marks, Fossi wins. Not because it's mind-blowingly good, but simply because it oozes character. And these days it's rare to find a $10 wine that dares to be different. It's also rare to find a bottle of wine with a label that both the proletariat and feminists will find endearing. Fossi Rosso is table wine in its true form, a non-vintage mix of all the reds—probably left over from making the good stuff—but damn if it doesn't work.

 turkey legs

 strong and stinky

 patio/picnic, wine geek

FOSSI ROSSO

VINO DA TAVOLA ROSSO
RED TABLE WINE
BOTTLED BY
CASA VINICOLA FOSSI DUILIO
FIESOLE - ITALIA
PRODUCT OF ITALY
750 ML   ALC 12% BY VOL

Rosso
Italy
$9.95

mezzomondo

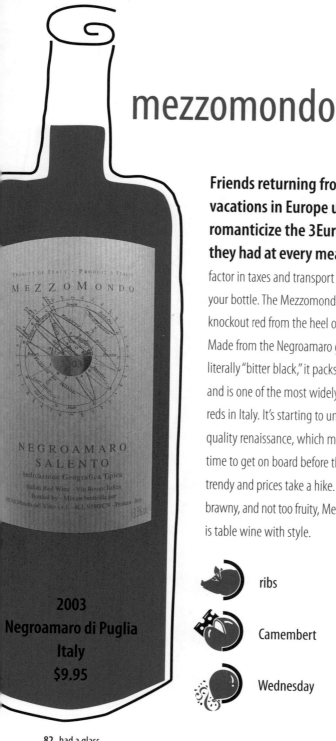

**2003
Negroamaro di Puglia
Italy
$9.95**

Friends returning from vacations in Europe usually romanticize the 3Euro wines they had at every meal. Well, factor in taxes and transport and here's your bottle. The Mezzomondo is a knockout red from the heel of Italy. Made from the Negroamaro grape, literally "bitter black," it packs a punch and is one of the most widely planted reds in Italy. It's starting to undergo a quality renaissance, which means it's time to get on board before things get trendy and prices take a hike. Dark ruby, brawny, and not too fruity, Mezzomondo is table wine with style.

 ribs

 Camembert

 Wednesday

finca los primos

Malbec is Merlot's alter ego with its rich, soft fruit flavours, but then it walks on the wild side with brambly black-currants, tanned leather, and a rustic rear end. If this appeals to you, this is your wine. Full of ripe fruit and wood spice as well as a hint of smokiness, it begs to be paired with the traditional grilled meats of the high plains. After all, four out of five gauchos agree: it's the darling red of Argentina.

 grilled T-bone

 winter warmer, beginner

SAN RAFAEL

FINCA
LOS PRIMOS

ARGENTINA

MALBEC

PRODUCIDO Y FRACCIONADO POR
VALENTIN BIANCHI SACIF, CTE. TORRES 500
SAN RAFAEL, MENDOZA
ESTABLECIMIENTO N° K-71831
EXPORTADOR N° K-87503

14% alc./vol.   750ml

2003
Malbec
Argentina
$9.95

The dye used to stamp the grade on meat is made from grape skins. Yes, it's edible.

la bastide

PRODUIT DE FRANCE

2004

LA BASTIDE

Vin de Pays de l'Herault

MIS EN BOUTEILLE
À LA PROPRIÉTÉ

Alc. 12.5 by vol. 750 ml

VIN ROUGE
RED WINE

PRODUCT OF FRANCE

**2003
Vin de Pays de l'Herault
France
$9.99**

Bastide takes bargain-hunting to the next level with its true-value red from the hinterlands of France's wine country. Southern France is heralded as the jackpot for your cheap drinking pleasures, but take it from us: there are some real nasties out there. This one delivers flavours of plum, strawberry, and semi-sweet chocolate. Plastic cork, instead of wood, means no cork-tainted wine. Plastic cork also means drink now. (You won't find synthetic plugs in bottles meant for the cellar.)

 ratatouille

 Wednesday, BYO

Get Closure Real corks look great, but 1 in 20 contain a compound that deadens the wine's flavour. Synthetic corks and screwcaps avoid the cork-taint—and the wine can be opened with just as much romance.

phoque rouge

If your "personal brand" doesn't include a personally selected table wine, here's a worthy contender. Table wine should be cheap, versatile, and outgoing. Enter Phoque Rouge. A blend of Syrah and Grenache, this garnet-coloured wine bursts with berrylicious fruit, orange rind, and tea leaf. Its easy-drinking style makes it a worthy partner for most meals, and the screwcap bottle says "drink me now."

 roast chicken

 grilled halibut

 patio/picnic, romance

Phoque rouge

VIN DE PAYS DES COTEAUX
DES BARONNIES

SIGNATURES DU SUD

**2003
Coteaux des Baronnies
France
$9.99**

josé maria da fonseca

Looks like they did away with some of the kinks of the previous vintage. Less funk, more fruit: the 00 Periquita is raspberries, plum, and tobacco leaf. But lovers of the old Portuguese styling fear not. They haven't forgotten the farm: it's like walking through a barn on a warm spring afternoon, the air fresh with the smell of healthy animals. "Rustic" might be one way to put it, but Periquita's got character out the wazoo. Remarkable for the small amount of cash they charge.

 ham

 Swiss

 wine geek, rock out

**2000
Periquita
Portugal
$10.90**

codici

It's like every Italian wine is jockeying for that sweet spot price point—delivering big taste for little dollar. And while success can be judged on many fronts, let's put an end to donut wines (juicy upfront and oaky in the rear, but with a flavour hole in the middle) and say hello to something inexpensive but serious like Codici. It's got hefty flavour, good balance, great price, and doesn't succumb to the doughy trappings of its contemporaries.

 ham hocks

 Gorgonzola

 BYO, rock out

CODICI

SALENTO
INDICAZIONE GEOGRAFICA TIPICA
ROSSO 2002

2002
Rosso
Italy
$11.50

penascal

PENASCAL

RED WINE - TEMPRANILLO - VIN ROUGE

2001
Tempranillo
Spain
$11.99

A few years ago we rented a car and drove across the Spanish expanse that is Castilla y León. There are a handful of well-recognized wine areas there—Ribera del Duero, Rueda, Toro—but otherwise we just kept staring through the windshield at bulk-wine land. Lots and lots of wine from lots and lots of vines is often unremarkable, but once in a while the wine is like the Penascal Tempranillo. At a great price, you get smoky Bing cherries and dusty earth aromas, fruit flavours that please the palate, and soft tannins, all in a well-balanced package.

 chili

 baked chops

 BYO, beginner

pascual toso

Originally a grape associated with Bordeaux and south-western France (a.k.a. Cot), a modern Malbec renaissance is taking place in Argentina.

The Toso Malbec has the great, brooding, purple-black colour typical of Malbec, with aromas of plum, vanilla, and a hint of violets. This is a suitably rich, plum- and berry-tasting wine that finishes with firm tannins, plenty of oak, and nuances of chocolate-covered coffee beans. A great example of Malbec at this price.

 roast

 grilled chops

 winter warmer, romance

2003
Malbec
Argentina
$11.99

de bortoli

AUSTRALIA
DE BORTOLI
Riverina
SHIRAZ
2003
WINE OF AUSTRALIA

2003
Shiraz
"DB"
Australia
$11.99

It's not an easy job navigating your way through the veritable sea of mundane, bulk-produced red wine to something worth a second whiff. You'd be shocked to hear the gory details of how we had to sip—and spit—through gallons of wine to find the stuff worth swallowing. So we're down on cheap reds when suddenly we're swept off our feet by the DB Shiraz, an expertly balanced wine with aromas of blueberries and bacon. Fresh plums and raspberries round out the flavour bag.

 pepper steak

 baked yams

 Wednesday, BYO

tsantali

The Tsantali Rapsani finds a spot in this book because it's not fruit juice, it's not cream soda, and it's not an over-oaked barrel child. Instead it's a solid, serious wine with ample character spawning heady herb and smoke aromas. It comes from properly ripe fruit and shows this with full flavour and a long finish.

 suckling pig

 mushroom farfalle

 wine geek

2001
Rapsani
Greece
$12.45

Calorie counters: Wine has about the same caloric count as an equal-sized glass of grape juice.

boutari

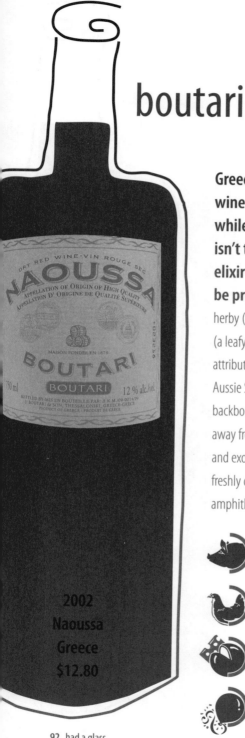

Greece is one of the oldest wine-producing regions, and while the Boutari Naoussa isn't the amphora-stored elixir of yore, Dionysus would be proud of this wine. Savoury, herby (sage and thyme), pickled shiso (a leafy Japanese herb)—these aren't attributes you'll find in your everyday Aussie Shiraz. They are, however, the backbone of this Naoussa, which leans away from fruity and towards earthy and exotic. In the right context (BBQ, freshly conquered game meat, at an amphitheatre) this wine rocks.

2002
Naoussa
Greece
$12.80

 pot roast

 chicken salad

 Gruyère

 wine geek, patio/picnic

bodegas castaño

Coming across this wine a few years back was a revelation.
Putting so much potent oomph into one bottle (at such a nice price) is near criminal. Then it was ten bucks. Now it has a new label and the price tag has inflated, but it's still a great bargain. The Monastrell grape thrives in Spain's hot vineyards. In the wrong hands it becomes blowsy, but Castaño keeps things in check, serving up intense overtures of blackberry, green olive, and scorched earth. It's inky, bold, and grippy—the wine equivalent of the little black dress.

 marinated and grilled

 eggplant parmigiana

 Manchego

 winter warmer, Wednesday

2003

CASTAÑO

2003

MONASTRELL

YECLA

2003
Monastrell
Spain
$12.95

j. bouchon

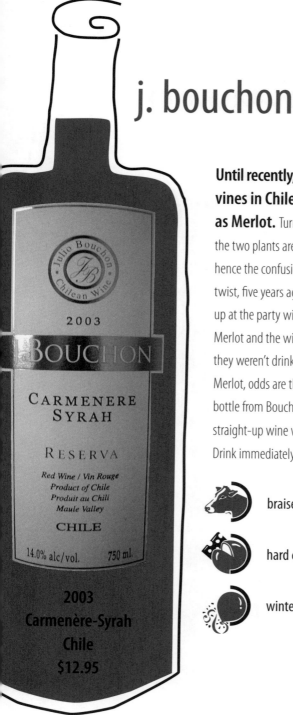

2003

BOUCHON

CARMENERE
SYRAH

RESERVA

Red Wine / Vin Rouge
Product of Chile
Produit au Chili
Maule Valley

CHILE

14.0% alc/vol.   750 ml.

2003
Carmenère-Syrah
Chile
$12.95

Until recently, most Carmenère vines in Chile were mistaken as Merlot. Turns out the leaves of the two plants are strikingly similar, hence the confusion. So in a funny twist, five years ago when you showed up at the party with a bottle of Chilean Merlot and the wine snobs protested they weren't drinking any more f'ing Merlot, odds are they weren't. Get this bottle from Bouchon for a plump, juicy, straight-up wine with a spicy twist. Drink immediately.

 braised

 hard cheese

winter warmer, rock out

trivento

There's a load of wine adjectives out there that inevitably make their way into wine writing—for better or for worse. Some are useful, some are wine bunk. We've heard "toilet bowl" and "wet cement," "chihuahua," and "hockey bag." If you Google "aroma wheel" you'll find A.C. Noble's cheat sheet, a handy sidekick if you're stuck for adjectives. Of course it's not an infinite list, and sure enough it's missing the words that describe this delectable Trivento Cab-Malbec: leather chaps.

 oxtail stew

 pecorino

 winter warmer, Wednesday

2002
Cabernet-Malbec
"Reserve"
Argentina
$12.95

zunio

2002
ZUNIO
OLD VINES
ZINFANDEL
LODI

ALC. 14.5% BY VOL./750 ML
RED WINE/VIN ROUGE   PRODUCT OF U.S.A./PRODUIT DES E.U.

2002
Zinfandel
California
$12.99

The number-one wine party trick is blind tasting. Here's when you impress your friends by guessing what wine is in your glass using only the information gathered by your sensory faculties. It's a worthless, slightly obnoxious thing to do, yet it holds credence in wine circles. Go figure. Anyhow, if you're blind tasting, and if the wine is red and smells unmistakably like strawberry pie, then put your money on California Zinfandel. The Zunio is a great example; also note raspberry juice concentrate and still more strawberries.

 minestrone

 chocolate

 on its own

 winter warmer, beginner

viu manent

Malbec's the dark and hand-some stranger you've been secretly wanting in your life.
More mysterious and sexy than Merlot, Malbec typically offers up its plump plum and dark berry flavours with a healthy dose of earth and gaminess. At least that's how most Malbecs from Argentina appear. Across the Andes in Chile's Central Valley, family-run Viu Manent has toned down the rustic and played up the fruit. The result is a rich, chocolate, and spicy plum Malbec that's plusher than 600-count Frette.

 stew

 chops

 smoked Gouda

 romance, Wednesday

ESTATE BOTTLED

VIU MANENT

MALBEC

COLCHAGUA VALLEY-CHILE

2 0 0 4

MIGUEL VIU MANENT · COLCHAGUA - CHILE

**2004
Malbec
Chile
$12.99**

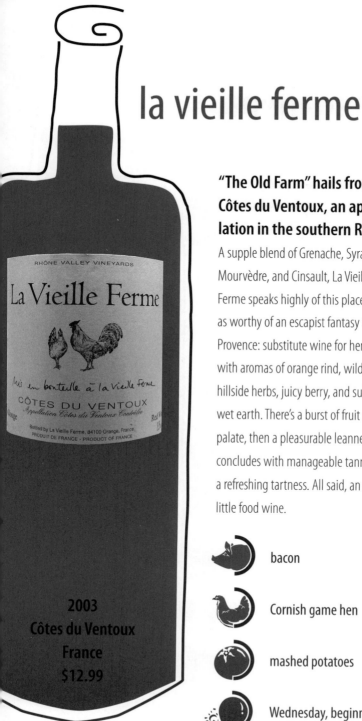

la vieille ferme

"The Old Farm" hails from Côtes du Ventoux, an appellation in the southern Rhône.

A supple blend of Grenache, Syrah, Mourvèdre, and Cinsault, La Vieille Ferme speaks highly of this place (it's as worthy of an escapist fantasy as Provence: substitute wine for herbs) with aromas of orange rind, wild hillside herbs, juicy berry, and subtle wet earth. There's a burst of fruit on the palate, then a pleasurable leanness that concludes with manageable tannins and a refreshing tartness. All said, an elegant little food wine.

2003
Côtes du Ventoux
France
$12.99

 bacon

 Cornish game hen

 mashed potatoes

 Wednesday, beginner

delicato

Delicato makes an endearing Shiraz from the up-and-coming Lodi region in California. Sadly, while there's not a lot of surfing— or surfer girls—in inland Lodi, what you do get are lots of ripening rays for the grapes to soak in. The Shiraz shows a nicely composed nose of blueberry fruit alongside a floral, perfumy nuance characteristic of the grape. Keep an eye out for a keen peppery kick in this wine's medium-long finish, another distinguishing trademark of Shiraz. Easily likeable in its smoothness and generous fruit flavours, it's a fetching drink.

 burgers

 on its own

 Wednesday, BYO, beginner

2002
Shiraz
California
$13.99

Methyphobia is the fear of alcohol.

miral monte

Joven = young wine, bottled early. Here's the polar opposite of those Spanish Reservas and Gran Reservas that sit languidly around the winery (Reservas: 3 years, GRs: 5) in oak barrels and steel bins while they mature. Joven is in the bottle and out the door—and, if it's the Miral Monte, hopefully right on to your dinner table. This wine busts out youthful aromas of plum and blackberry fruit over a smoky and earthy backdrop. We think that everyone should experience drinking an older, well-aged wine; everyone should also experience this.

2003
Toro Joven
Spain
$13.99

 steak and fries

 Saint Paulin

 on its own

 winter warmer

rosemount

There's nothing like a U-pick romp through the strawberry patch, close and personal with all that fresh fruit and earth. Trouble is, berry season is short-lived. To experience the occasion year-round, crack open a bottle of Rosemount's Shiraz Grenache and inhale the "Grenache perfume," a lifted berry aromatic that balances ripe fruit and flowers. It's bursting with berries, vanilla, and a spicy floral (nasturtium) nose that will put a smile on any imbiber's lips, with just enough dusty earth to round out the illusion. Things stay fruity until the rich, spicy characters of Syrah meld into the mix.

 roast chicken with herbs

 chili

 St. Nectare

 romance, Wednesday

2003
Shiraz-Grenache
"Diamond Label"
Australia
$13.99

viña albali

The Valdepeñas wine region of Spain is hugged by the southern end of its goliath neighbour, La Mancha. In its sheer size, La Mancha single-handedly supports a vast majority of Spanish wine culture. The non-stop vines sit on a high plateau dead-centre in the middle of the continent where they're baked by summer sun and parched due to minute rainfall. Hot heat. The Albali is fragrant with overripe cherry and woodspice aromas. Look for hints of mocha, bacon, and tobacco that add complexity to the wine, setting it apart from its peers.

 prime rib

 vegetable paella

 Castellano

 winter warmer, rock out

VIÑA
ALBALI
RESERVA
RED WINE - VIN ROUGE
1999

IMPORTER: MARBE OF CANADA

PRODUCT OF SPAIN · PRODUIT D'ESPAGNE

Viña Albali Reservas

1999
Valdepeñas Reserva
Spain
$14.90

montes

Be that Chilean gigolo: pop the cork on a bottle of Montes Cab Sauv, pick up a copy of Pablo Neruda's "Ode to Wine," pile up the kindling, and cook up some empanadas. As you recite the fabled poet's words, the wine's ruby brilliance will twinkle in the firelight: "My darling, suddenly/the line of your hip/becomes the brimming curve/of the wine goblet . . ." Take a sip, you Latin lover. Even if you don't get anywhere, your lips will delight in flavours of ripe blackcurrant, vanilla, and smoky toastiness.

 tenderloin

 aged cheddar

 beginner, cellar

**2004
Cabernet Sauvignon
Chile
$14.95**

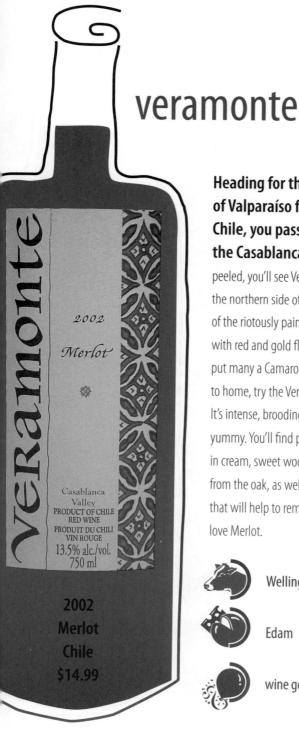

veramonte

Heading for the coastal city of Valparaíso from Santiago, Chile, you pass right through the Casablanca Valley. Eyes peeled, you'll see Veramonte's winery off the northern side of Ruta 68. Take one of the riotously painted private buses, with red and gold flames that would put many a Camaro to shame. Closer to home, try the Veramonte Merlot. It's intense, brooding, rich, and entirely yummy. You'll find plum and ripe berries in cream, sweet wood spice and clove from the oak, as well as a suave finish that will help to remind why you can still love Merlot.

 Wellington

 Edam

 wine geek, winter warmer

2002
Merlot
Chile
$14.99

tocornal

The scenario: Party

The setup: Wine needed

The strategy: Quantity counts, but with some semblance of quality

The answer: Tocornal! This Cab Merlot pleases crowds with style. Lots of berries and bramble float out of the glass, while taste-wise the Tocornal is soft, fruity, and very drinkable. Note: Tocornal comes only in a magnum (1.5 litres).

 meatloaf

 roast

 BYO

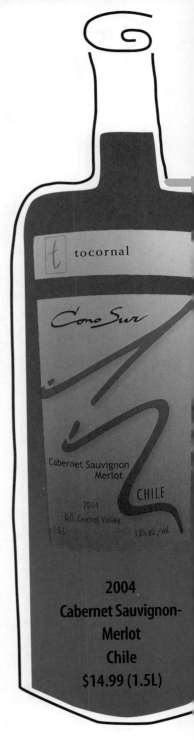

2004
Cabernet Sauvignon-
Merlot
Chile
$14.99 (1.5L)

Size matters: Beringer's Maximus is the world's largest wine bottle, holding over 173 bottles of Cabernet Sauvignon.

bouchard aîné & fils

Pinossimo
PINOT NOIR

DEPUIS 1750
BOUCHARD AÎNÉ & FILS
FRANCE
VIN · WINE · PRODUIT DE FRANCE · PRODUCT OF FRANCE

2003
Pinot Noir
"Pinossimo"
France
$14.99

Isak Dinesen, of *Out of Africa* fame, once said "… there are many ways to the recognition of truth, and Burgundy is one of them." We agree, but given the current price of a good bottle of Burgundy (the home of Pinot Noir), we've been searching for truth in other domains. Bouchard Aîné brings its Burgundy know-how to the more affordable vineyards of southern France to make their Pinossimo. Inside the modern-look bottle you'll find a modern French Pinot: fruity strawberry and orange peel with a spicy oak finish.

 pheasant

 lentil lasagna

 bouillabaisse

 patio/picnic

le bombarde

If hip-hop had a sense of humour, rappers would gather in their ciphers swigging "Le Bombarde." The grape is Cannonau, le bombarde roughly translates as "the cannons," and the futurist label shows duelling munitions. It's da proverbial bomb and a great little bottle of wine—soft and smooth, fruity and spicy, straightforward and keeping it real.

 ham sandwich

 wings

 BBQ salmon

 wine geek, BYO

**2003
Cannonau di Sardegna
Italy
$14.99**

di majo norante

Here's a stripped-down yet strapping Sangiovese from Di Majo, one of a handful of organic Italians we see on our shelves. It delivers a load of cherry fruit backed by some dry herbs and a touch of old wood; nothing blousy or half-assed about this Sangio—it's straight-up, offering a great look at the grape in all its glory. If you're after a fruit bomb, go shopping somewhere else; this is real wine and not some pop tart cop-out.

 tomato pasta

 Toscanello

 Wednesday, romance

**2002
Sangiovese
Italy
$14.99**

flagstone

Here's a wine for blend fetishists. Flagstone has squeezed eight cultivars (grape varieties) into their "Backchat Blend." For number crunchers out there, we're talking 40 percent Cabernet Sauvignon, 22 percent Shiraz, 15 percent Merlot, 9 percent Pinotage, 4 percent Pinot Noir, 4 percent Tinta Barocca, 4 percent Sauvignon Blanc, and 2 percent Cabernet Franc. The result of this whacko mix is an eminently drinkable, entirely enjoyable red. A smooth operator, The Backchat Blend is a rich, chocolatey wine that shouts crowd pleaser.

 stroganoff

 Parmigiano Reggiano

 winter warmer, BYO

**2002
Cellar Hand
"The Backchat Blend"
South Africa
$14.99**

mad dogs & englishmen

More hot wine from hot Spain! It cooks in southern Spain and the proof's in the pudding. Ultra-ripe and sweet fruit aromas of blueberries and baked sugar plums dominate this blend. Despite the big flavours, however, there's great balance and integrity here, including a lip-smacking, savoury-tart finish that keeps everything on the up-and-up. Yes, there's a dog (a Jack Russell terrier, if we're not mistaken) on the bottle, but before you dis animal labels, we suggest you try the MD&E.

 on its own

 BYO, rock out

**2003
Monastrell-Shiraz-
Cabernet Sauvignon
Spain
$14.99**

Sip this while watching the classic rockumentary *Joe Cocker: Mad Dogs and Englishmen*. But if Leon Russell's appearance in the movie is why there's a Jack Russell on the wine label, we must wonder why there's no Cocker Spaniel, too.

mission hill

The major problem with Pinot Noir is the prohibitive price. If you want a good bottle, it's going to cost you. So, we get giddy when we find a cheap bottle that shows true Pinot character. Thank you, Mission Hill. Their "Five Vineyards" walks the fine Pinot line between fruitiness and earthiness, the yin/yang character that enraptures Pinot-philes. Great cherry aromas mesh with a woodsiness reminiscent of a forest interpretative hike. A supple, silky example of the Tao of Pinot.

 duck

 salmon

 wine geek, beginner

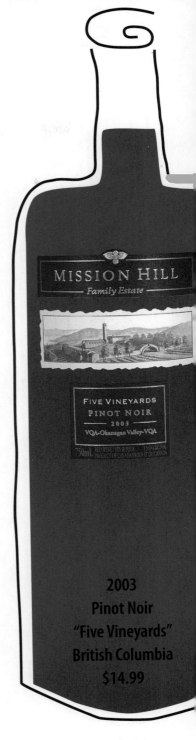

**2003
Pinot Noir
"Five Vineyards"
British Columbia
$14.99**

fontanafredda

Dr. Phil told us it's not important where you come from, but rather where "you're at."

Thank God Dr. Phil isn't a wine critic. Wines should be made to reflect the land they're from, not follow some generic flavour profile. This is the essence of terroir. The Fontanafredda tastes like northern Italy. It's colder up there close to the Alps, and the grapes don't ripen into the fruit bombs of hotter climes. The Fontanafredda expresses this to a T: reserved fruit, grainy tannins, lighter body, and a refreshing finish. Delicious, but Dr. Phil also told us drinking the whole bottle isn't going to solve our problems.

FONTANAFREDDA

BARBERA D'ALBA
DENOMINAZIONE DI ORIGINE CONTROLLATA
APPELLATION D'ORIGINE CONTROLÉE

DRY RED WINE · VIN ROUGE SEC
2002

IMBOTTIGLIATO ALL'ORIGINE · EMBOUTEILLE PAR FONTANAFREDDA · SERRALUNGA D'ALBA · ITALY · ITALIE
PRODUCT OF ITALY · PRODUIT D'ITALIE

**2003
Barbera d'Alba
Italy
$15.49**

 Bourguignon, Italian style

 baked eggplant

 patio/picnic, wine geek

tinhorn creek

Tinhorn Creek peeks out from a sloping hill in Oliver to sweeping valley vistas below.

This certifiable pocket desert in the south Okanagan is arguably the best place to grow red grapes in Canada, and when done right you get a bottle like this Cabernet Franc. Tinhorn has tamed this grape, creating a wine with attractive berry and tobacco-leaf aromas, and a BIG, intense palate of fruit and oak. It's great now—a little rough around the edges for those who like it that way—and the wine will only improve if you give it a few years.

 rib roast

 eggplant gratin

 Manchego

 winter warmer, cellar

2002
Cabernet Franc
British Columbia
$15.95

chapoutier

2003

BILA-HAUT

CÔTES DU ROUSSILLON
APPELLATION CÔTES DU ROUSSILLON CONTRÔLÉE

MIS EN BOUTEILLE PAR M. CHAPOUTIER
M. CHAPOUTIER
26600 TAIN · FRANCE

PRODUIT DE FRANCE · PRODUCE OF FRANCE

**2003
Côtes du Roussillon
Villages "Bila Haut"
France
$16.90**

Organic wine gets slagged because for so long it sucked.

Farmers were busy dropping pesticide bombs on their vineyards because there was little interest in organic farming and no excitement in the wines. The good news is, we're getting smarter. There's value now in these organic grapes— not only because they're drug-free, but because we're learning how a natural vineyard makes good fruit. Here Chapoutier can smile because they've been biodynamic (organic turned up a notch) for years and making fine, fine wine.

 cutlets

 stuffed chicken thighs

 portobello tortellini

 picnic, Wednesday

The latest spa treatment is vinotherapy—soaking in a bathtub full of wine.

st. hallett

Synergy! Shiraz + Grenache + Mourvèdre + Touriga Nacional = Gamekeeper's Reserve. The grapes are all great solo performers, but here they meld into an authoritative four-part harmony that would make any barbershop quartet proud. The Shiraz brings mulberry fruit and a white pepper spiciness, while the Grenache shines through with lifted berry aromatics. The Mourvèdre grounds things with a firm earthiness, and the Touriga provides a unique kick in the rear. There's no "I" in Gamekeeper's Reserve; this is bottled teamwork.

 baseball steak

 chocolate

 winter warmer, BYO, rock out

2003
Gamekeeper's Reserve
Australia
$16.95

2001
Toscana
Italy
$16.95

monte antico

Don't be misled by the rustic label—Monte Antico is one mod Chianti. The Italians know good style and here's bottled proof. The wine stays true to its Sangiovese roots. Black cherry and vanilla dominate, counter-balanced by pencil shavings and tealeaf. The rich mid-palate leads to a tart, grippy finish that screams for tomato sauce—a classic Tuscan food and wine match.

 pork osso bucco

 risotto

 Provolone

 BYO, beginner

beyerskloof

Pinotage is like cauliflower and gangsta rap: you either love it or hate it—there's no fence-sitting. Given this, it's not surprising that Pinotage proponents display a daring passion for their beloved grape. Consider Beyerskloof: a Pinotage grape leaf graces their winery logo, they print Pinotage propaganda T-shirts, hell, they even helped develop a Pinotage ice cream. Thankfully, they back up their obsession with a bottle like this. We dare you to try it.

 BBQ sauce

 brie

 wine geek, rock out

WINE OF SOUTH AFRICA

BEYERSKLOOF

PINOTAGE

2003

14.0% Vol   WINE OF ORIGIN   750 ml
STELLENBOSCH

**2003
Pinotage
South Africa
$16.99**

nk'mip cellars

**2003
Pinot Noir
British Columbia
$16.99**

Just when you thought French labels were hard to pronounce, along comes Nk'Mip. For the record, it's pronounced enk-meep, and this is North America's first Aboriginal-owned-and-operated winery. Their Pinot Noir is wonderfully silky and of the modern, fruit-forward persuasion. Gobs of cherry and rhubarb characterize both the aromas and flavours of the wine, and the finish follows through suave. File under juicy.

 chicken drumstick

 ratatouille

 on its own

 picnic, romance, aperitif

Wine Tunes: Jay Z's "The Black Album"

a-mano

Primitivo meet Zinfandel. Zin meet Prim. Long-lost cousins, the Italian Primitivo and California Zinfandel make a reunion in Mark Shannon's A-Mano. No, there's none of the Cali grape in here—it's 100% Italian Stallion—but Shannon crafts Primitivo perfectly in this ridiculously well-priced red. Suggestions of the California connection manifest as aromas of impossibly ripe, sun-baked strawberries, but best of all Shannon keeps the barnyard out of the wine. To clarify: too many Primitivos smell like manure, but the A-Mano stays clean and gives you a taste of the good stuff.

 New York steak

 on its own

 romance, winter warmer

2002
Primitivo
Italy
$17.45

Wine Tunes: Willie Bobo's "Juicy"

castillo de molina

2002
Cabernet Sauvignon
"Reserve"
Chile
$17.55

Here's Bordeaux on a good day, and it's from Chile. The Castillo de Molina is a fine example of Chile's prowess with classic red grapes. This Cab Sauv wafts amazing berry and cassis aromas, which mingle with butterscotch and vanilla from the oak barrels used for ageing. Rich and robust, the Molina has the flavours Cab fans have come to love. A big, lengthy finish with hefty tannins sums things up. If anything, a few more years in the bottle will mellow this wine and have the French quivering in their chateaux.

 filet mignon

 chocolate

 Camembert

 BYO, cellar

porcupine ridge

Shoulder pads have their place. Things got a little out of control with the foam wedges that ran amok in the 80s but, still, a little structure and brawn can be a good look. The Porcupine Ridge is Syrah with shoulder pads. Ripe, juicy blackberry and blueberry await, but the flavours are delivered in a package that highlights well-balanced elegance. Porcupine Ridge deftly walks the fruit-forward/terroir-driven tightrope. A perfect wine to swing under the arm of that pinstripe power suit!

 braised short-ribs

 on its own

 rock out

2003
Syrah
South Africa
$17.99

columbia crest

2002

COLUMBIA·CREST
Two Vines

SHIRAZ
COLUMBIA VALLEY

2002
Shiraz "Two Vines"
Washington
$17.99

The "Two Vines" supposedly pays homage to the unique grape trellising used throughout Washington's Columbia Valley, but we know better. We figure it's a veiled attempt at multilateral Shiraz relations. Or a unilateral front on Australia, CC usurping the Aussies at their own Shiraz game with a dead ringer. Having recently rejigged their bottles from Syrah to the more consumer-friendly Shiraz, Columbia Crest is on to ripe, juicy, oaky pastures. It's Oz Shiraz with a Yank accent.

 pepper steak

 on its own

 winter warmer, beginner

barone ricasoli

Buying inexpensive Chianti is like playing Minesweeper.
So many of these red wines bomb so that after a couple of tries you go back to solitaire. The fact of the matter is, for under $20 there are so many crappy Chiantis that we don't blame anyone for quitting the game. But we love a solid, serious Chianti and that's why we love the Ricasoli. Say goodbye to unripe cherries and hello to prunes and liquorice, tobacco, and tilled earth. Get serious about Chianti, and Chianti will get serious about you.

 brisket with prunes

 Parmigiano Reggiano

 romance, winter warmer

2002
Chianti
Italy
$18.90

perrin

2001
Côtes du Rhône
"Reserve"
France
$18.99

There was a time when Côtes du Rhône was hailed as the red wine saviour of France.

When Bordeaux became big money and Beaujolais got all nouveau, CdR gave people a reason to buy French. But these days? With CdR on everyone's drink list, it's hard to find something decent sub $20. A saving grace is the Perrin Reserve, a serious Côtes du Rhône true to form with dusty raspberries and dry earthiness, orange peel and black cherries.

 coq au vin

 roasted veggies

 Morbier

 wine geek, BYO

inniskillin

Chuck away the map, colour outside the lines, and live life to the fullest. This Inni is a rich BC red that makes no excuses. Mocha and chocolate dominate, mingling with juicy berry and vanilla bean. There are lots of tannins here and they linger on forever, making this a good candidate to put down for a few years. We do recommend this Cab Sauv be a part of a balanced meal, preferably something four-legged and protein-based, though if you don't swing that way, we'll turn a blind eye to tofurkey.

 prime rib

 chocolate

 romance, cellar

**2003
Cabernet Sauvignon
"Dark Horse Vineyard"
British Columbia
$19.99**

quinta do crasto

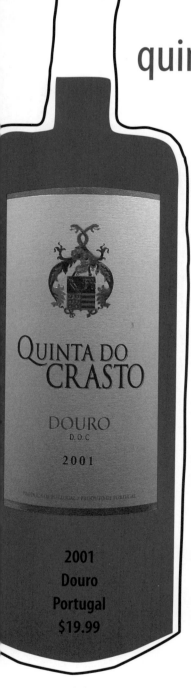

2001
Douro
Portugal
$19.99

The absolutely lame thing about wine cellars is A) you're supposed to keep wine in them for a long time and B) the wine you're supposed to keep is always so freaking expensive. So you lay all this cash down for something that's ready to drink around the time you're dead. And if you manage to get undead to drink it, it won't be any fun because no one likes a drunk zombie. Instead, spend $60 on three bottles of this Crasto. Drink one now because it's the best Portuguese wine in this book. Put the other two in your closet and drink one next year and one the year after that.

 steak Diane

 brie

 rock out, cellar

bonny doon

This is wine gonzo. The glaring red screwcap and hyperkinetic Ralph Steadman-illustrated label dare you onwards. You crack the cap. Inside, the Blagueurs continues its hedonistic taunt. Stinky in a comforting way, this is serious Syrah—blooming flowers in rich topsoil. It's intense and spicy as all get-out, with a lengthy, lingering finish. Better bring your toothbrush—the tannins will paint your pucker purple. Not for sissy wine drinkers.

 on its own

 wine geek, rock out

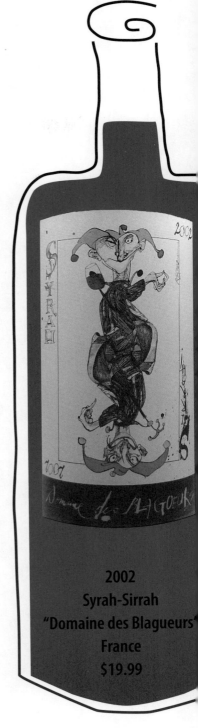

2002
Syrah-Sirrah
"Domaine des Blagueurs"
France
$19.99

had a glass

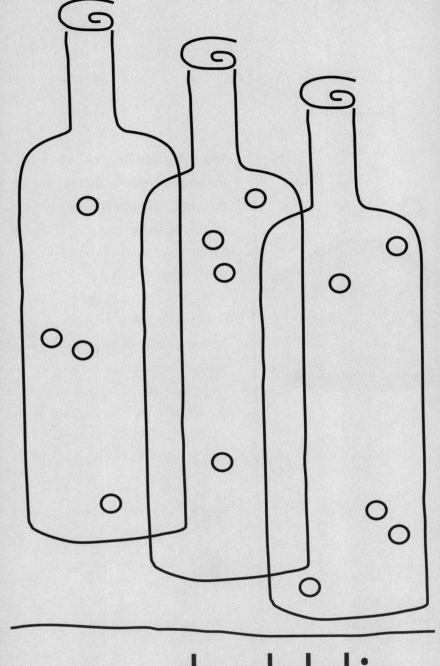

the bubblies

cook's

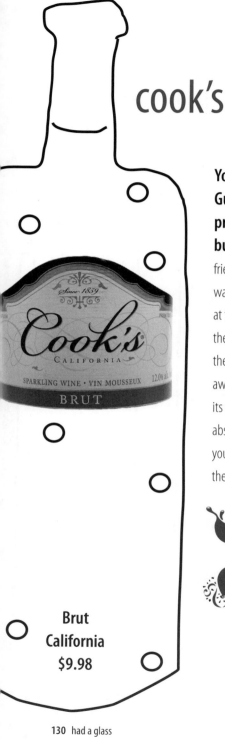

**Brut
California
$9.98**

Your inner Boy Scout or Girl Guide insists you're always prepared with a bottle of bubbly on hand. And if your friends are anything like ours, you might want to keep an inexpensive decoy at the ready. For our money, Cook's is the best bubbly under ten bucks on the shelves. It's not going to win any awards, it's not going to impress with its complexity, but it's cheap, dry, and absolutely perfect for those times when you crave a low-brow Champer to keep the night going (or start the day right).

 on its own

 patio/picnic, Wednesday

marquis de la tour

Don't wait for a birthday or a new year to have a bottle of sparkling wine—bust out the bubble for any occasion.

That's what P. Diddy does, and it should be a lesson for us all. Of course the only bub he'd ever be caught in public with is Cristal and Dom, but when Puffy's chillin' at home, he's probably sipping a bottle of Marquis and watching his pocketbook. Without dropping a fifty-spot you get treated to plenty of bubbles so you can feel the part; enough of the Champer toastiness so that even your wine-savvy homies won't call foul.

 raw oysters

 pasta salad

 on its own

 beginner, aperitif

**Brut
France
$11.99**

segura viudas

BRUT RESERVA
This choice, vibrant cava is noted for balance and delicacy.
An enticing bouquet leads to crisp,
fresh flavors that linger on the palate.

CAVA

**Cava
"Brut Reserva"
Spain
$14.99**

Thanks to early stints in Barcelona, we came to love Cava before Champagne.

Cava—Spain's national sparkling wine—remains a favourite treat, and Segura Viudas is an old standby. Lemon meringue pie and a spritzy mousse characterize this bubbly with its light, refreshing palate. Not as customary as its French brethren, but the Catalonians like it a little surreal.

 fish and chips

 pan-fried scallops

 Thai noodles

 Wednesday, aperitif

banrock station

Sparkling Shiraz gets little attention outside of Australia.

Historically, wine geeks turn their noses up at red bubblies. Their loss. We found respect for sparkling Shiraz some years back in Melbourne, where a late-night bottle paired with hot dogs was the perfect pick-me-up after a hard day of touring. Banrock's SS embottles wine fun. Gobs of blackberries and boysenberries waft out of the glass. It's sweet but not cloying, fruity with a pleasant, earthy finish. This bottle will sing alongside anything dressed with ketchup.

 all-beef wieners

 chocolate

 on its own

 wine geek, romance, rock out

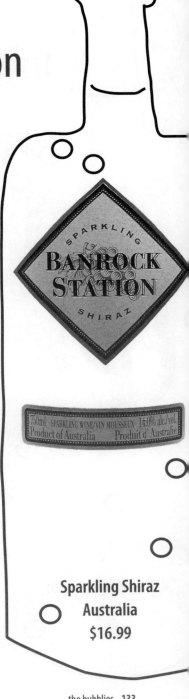

**Sparkling Shiraz
Australia
$16.99**

mionetto

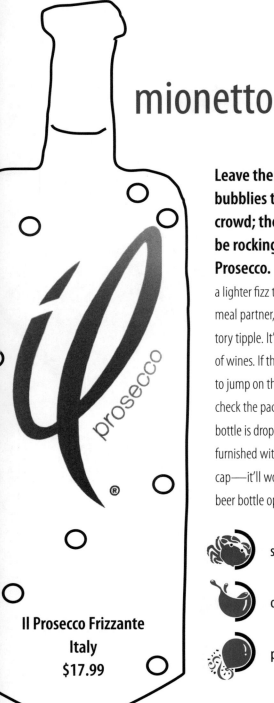

Leave the fancy French bubblies to the hip-hop crowd; the indie kids should be rocking bottles of Il Prosecco. It's fun, fresh, and fruity, a lighter fizz that works as an aperitif, a meal partner, a club sipper, or a celebratory tipple. It's the Swiss Army knife of wines. If that's not reason enough to jump on the Prosecco bandwagon, check the package: the curvaceous bottle is drop-dead gorgeous and even furnished with an alternative crown cap—it'll work fine with your old beer bottle opener collection.

 skewered

 on its own

 picnic, BYO, aperitif

Il Prosecco Frizzante
Italy
$17.99

Wine Tunes: AC Newman's "The Slow Wonder"

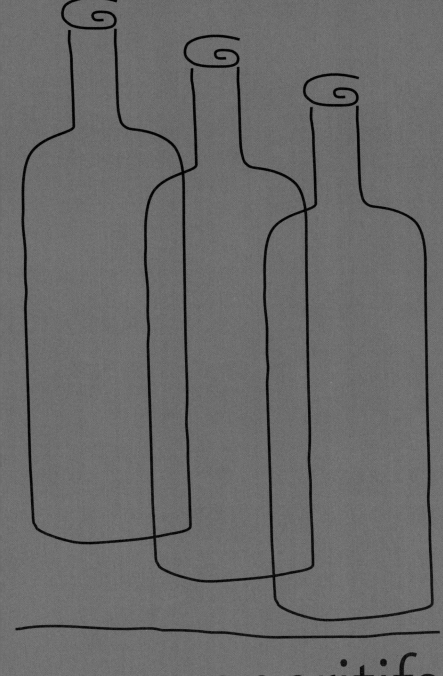

the aperitifs

lustau

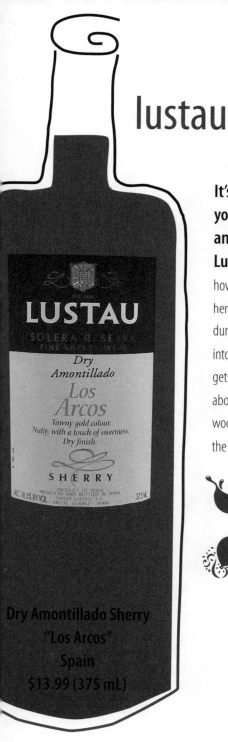

It's so freaking sexy when you go over to a girl's place and she offers you a glass of Lustau Amontillado. No matter how hot her low-risers are, how great her salon-coiffed locks look, when she dumps a couple of ounces of this nectar into a tulip-shaped glass, everything gets so much sexier. The hottest part about all this is the nutty, dried fruit, old wood smell of this sherry that spills into the room, setting the mood.

 on its own

 wine geek, aperitif

Dry Amontillado Sherry
"Los Arcos"
Spain
$13.99 (375 mL)

lillet

The inclusion of Lillet in this book is controversial. While not a wine per se, it's an aperitif based on wine. It's like those flavoured vodkas: you could squeeze some lemon juice into the real deal, but when push comes to shove is there anything wrong with reaching for the vodka citron? At the end of the day, there's nothing quite like opening the fridge and pouring a quick sip of sweetish Lillet to segue into the evening. The candied orange peel and tangerine flavours really get the gastrointestinal juices flowing.

 on its own

 aperitif, rock out

France
$16.98

gonzalez byass

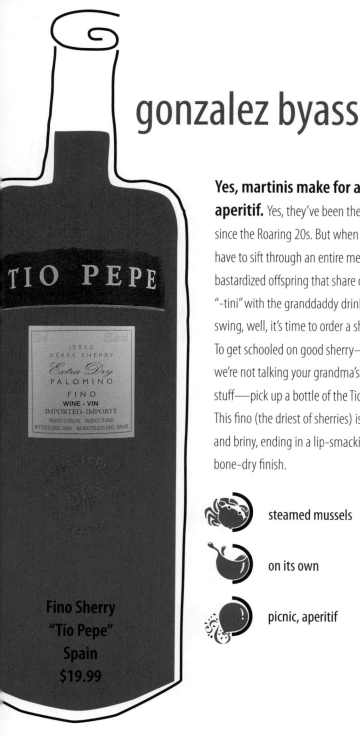

**Fino Sherry
"Tio Pepe"
Spain
$19.99**

Yes, martinis make for a swell aperitif. Yes, they've been the rage since the Roaring 20s. But when we have to sift through an entire menu of bastardized offspring that share only a "-tini" with the granddaddy drink of swing, well, it's time to order a sherry. To get schooled on good sherry—and we're not talking your grandma's sticky stuff—pick up a bottle of the Tio Pepe. This fino (the driest of sherries) is nutty and briny, ending in a lip-smacking, bone-dry finish.

 steamed mussels

 on its own

 picnic, aperitif

the desserts

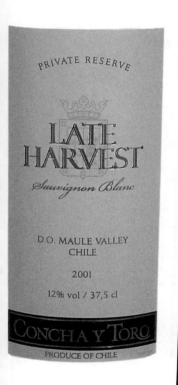

**Late Harvest
Sauvignon Blanc
Chile
$14.95 (375 mL)**

concha y toro

There's a reason why sweet wines are called dessert wines. We were at this wine dinner the other day—the kind where a different wine comes with each course—and everything was happening until some brainiac thought to serve a dry white wine with dessert. Taking a sip of a dry wine after a sugary mouthful of dessert makes the wine about as bland as a bunch of accountants talking balance sheets—or wine writers talking grapes, for that matter. A shame, because this LH Sauvignon Blanc is scrumptious tropical fruit and honey.

 on its own

 BYO, beginner

michele chiarlo

Every time we turn around there's a new way to woo your woman. Or seduce and destroy if you're Tom Cruise in *Magnolia*. Forget all the glossy magazine theories and Frank TJ Mackey seminars, Moscato d'Asti is the real deal. This off-dry, light-alcohol, slightly bubbly nectar chilled and served mid-afternoon or post-dinner is the uncontested palate libertine. Don't let the 5% alcohol fool you, Casanova—this is a bottled aphrodisiac.

 on its own

 romance

2002
Moscato d'Asti
"Nivole"
Italy
$17.27 (375 mL)

yalumba

Tawny Port
"Clocktower"
Australia
$17.99

Nothing says "nightcap" like a splash of port. Whether you do it with a wedge of cheese, fresh fruit, or solo, a tipple of the scrumptious dessert wine makes a perfect evening closer. But don't take too much time sipping the sweet—once a bottle of port is open it'll last for about a week and a half—two on the outside. With the Clocktower, though, you won't have to worry about expiration dates. It's that good, laced with unforgettable apricot and caramel flavours.

 blue

 on its own

 winter warmer, Wednesday

"It [drink] provokes the desire, but it takes away the performance." — Porter in *Macbeth*, Act II, Scene III

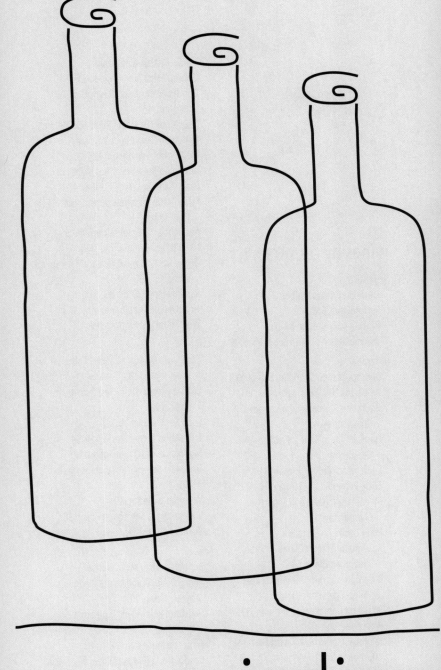

the indices

wines by country

Argentina

Finca Los Primos Malbec 83
Lurton Pinot Gris 43
Pascual Toso Malbec 89
Trivento "Reserve" Cabernet-Malbec 95

Australia

Banrock Station Sparkling Shiraz 133
De Bortoli "DB" Shiraz 90
Goundrey "Homestead Unwooded" Chardonnay 49
Hardys "Stamp Series" Riesling-Gewürztraminer 41
Lindemans "Bin 75" Riesling 44
Little Penguin Chardonnay 48
McWilliam's "Hanwood Estate" Chardonnay 62
Peter Lehmann Semillon 70
Rosemount Estate "Diamond Label" Sauvignon Blanc 63
Rosemount Estate "Diamond Label" Shiraz-Grenache 101
St. Hallett Gamekeeper's Reserve 115
Wynns Riesling 61
Yalumba "Clocktower" Tawny Port 142
Yalumba "Y Series" Viognier 72

Canada (British Columbia)

Calona "Artist Series" Pinot Gris 51
Gehringer Brothers "Classic Dry" Riesling 46
Gray Monk "Odyssey" Pinot Gris 74
Inniskillin "Dark Horse Vineyard" Cabernet Sauvignon 125
Inniskillin "Reserve" Pinot Blanc 50
Lang "Farm Reserve" Riesling 47
Mission Hill "Five Vineyards" Pinot Noir 111
Mt. Boucherie Gewürztraminer 56
Nk'Mip Cellars Pinot Noir 118
Quails' Gate "Limited Release" Chenin Blanc 67
Sandhill Pinot Blanc 65
Tinhorn Creek Cabernet Franc 113
Wild Goose Gewürztraminer 58

Chile

Castillo de Molina "Reserve" Cabernet Sauvignon 120
Concha y Toro Late Harvest Sauvignon Blanc 140
Cono Sur Viognier 42
J. Bouchon Carmenère-Syrah 94
Montes Cabernet Sauvignon 103
Tocornal Cabernet-Sauvignon-Merlot 105
Veramonte Merlot 104
Viña Tarapaca Sauvignon Blanc 38
Viu Manent Malbec 97

France

Bonnet-Huteau Muscadet Sur Lie 55
Bonny Doon "Domaine des Blagueurs" Syrah-Sirrah 127
Bouchard Aîne & Fils "Pinossimo" Pinot Noir 106
Cellier de Marrenon 77
Chapoutier "Bila Haut" Côtes de Roussillon Villages 114

wines by type

wines by food

Beef

A-Mano Primitivo 119
Banrock Station Sparkling 133
Barone Ricasoli Chianti 123
Castillo de Molina "Reserve" Cabernet
    Sauvignon 120
Columbia Crest "Two Vines" Shiraz 122
De Bortoli "DB" Shiraz 90
Delicato Shiraz 99
Finca Los Primos Malbec 83
Flagstone "The Backchat Blend"
    Cellar Hand 109
Fontanafredda Barbera d'Alba 112
Inniskillin "Dark Horse Vineyard"
    Cabernet Sauvignon 125
J. Bouchon Carmenère-Syrah 94
Lujuria 80
Miral Monte Toro Joven 100
Montes Cabernet Sauvignon 103
Pascual Toso Malbec 89
Penascal Tempranillo 88
Porcupine Ridge Syrah 121
Quinta do Crasto Duoro 126
St. Hallett Gamekeeper's Reserve 115
Tinhorn Creek Cabernet Franc 113
Tocornal Cabernet-Sauvignon-Merlot
    105

Trivento "Reserve" Cabernet-Malbec
    95
Veramonte Merlot 104
Viña Albali Valdepeñas Reserva 102
Viu Manent Malbec 97

Cheese

Barone Ricasoli Chianti 123
Beyerskloof Pinotage 117
Bodegas Castaño Monastrell 93
Boutari Naoussa 92
Castillo de Molina 120
Codici Rosso 87
Di Majo Norante Sangiovese 108
Dunavar "Connoisseur Collection"
    Pinot Gris 36
Fairview "Goats do Roam" White 60
Flagstone "The Backchat Blend"
    Cellar Hand 109
Fossi Rosso 81
J. Bouchon Carmenère-Syrah 94
José Maria da Fonseca Periquita 86
La Bastide 84
Lujuria 80
Lurton Pinot Gris 43
Mezzomondo Negroamaro di Puglia
    82
Miral Monte Toro Joven 100
Monte Antico Toscana 116
Montes Cabernet Sauvignon 103
Mt. Boucherie Gewürztraminer 56
Perrin "Reserve" Côtes du Rhône 124
Pfaffenheim Gewürztraminer 73
Quinta do Crasto Duoro 126
Rosemount Estate "Diamond Label"
    Sauvignon Blanc 101
Rosemount Estate "Diamond Label"
    Shiraz-Grenache 63
Tinhorn Creek Cabernet Franc 113
Trivento "Reserve" Cabernet-Malbec
    95

Poultry *(continued)*

Fairview "Goats do Roam" White 60
Fossi Rosso 81
Gray Monk "Odyssey" Pinot Gris 74
La Vieille Ferme 98
Lang "Farm Reserve" Riesling 47
Le Bombarde Cannonau di Sardegna 107
Little Penguin Chardonnay 48
Lorch Riesling 53
Lurton Pinot Gris 43
McWilliam's "Hanwood Estate" Chardonnay 62
Michel Laroche Chardonnay 68
Mission Hill "Five Vineyards" Pinot Noir 111
Nk'Mip Cellars Pinot Noir 118
Perrin "Reserve" Côtes du Rhône 124
Phoque Rouge 85
RH Phillips Chardonnay 52
Rosemount Estate "Diamond Label" Sauvignon Blanc 63
Rosemount Estate "Diamond Label" Shiraz-Grenache 101

Shellfish

Babich Sauvignon Blanc 71
Bertani Soave Classico Superiore 59
Bonnet-Huteau Muscadet Sur Lie 55
Cono Sur Viognier 42
Fazi Battaglia Verdicchio 57
Gehringer Brothers "Classic Dry" Riesling 46
Gonzales Byass "Tio Pepe" Fino Sherry 138
Gray Monk "Odyssey" Pinot Gris 74
Lindemans "Bin 75" Riesling 44
Lurton "Les Fumées Blanches" Sauvignon Blanc 45
Marqués de Riscal Rueda 69
Marquis de la Tour Brut 131

Mateus Rosé 76
Mionetto Il Prosecco Frizzante 134
Mt. Boucherie Gewürztraminer 56
Peter Lehmann Semillon 70
Quails' Gate "Limited Release" Chenin Blanc 67
Segura Viudas "Brut Reserva" Cava 132
Torres "Viña Esmeralda" 54
Viña Tarapaca Sauvignon Blanc 38
Wynns Riesling 61

Solo (on its own)

A-Mano Primitivo 119
Babich Sauvignon Blanc 71
Banrock Station Sparkling Shiraz 133
Blue Nun 37
Bonny Doon "Domaine des Blagueurs" Syrah-Sirrah 127
Calona "Artist Series" Pinot Gris 51
Columbia Crest "Two Vines" Shiraz 122
Concha y Toro Late Harvest Sauvignon Blanc 140
Cook's Brut 130
Delicato Shiraz 99
de Wetshof "Danie De Wet" Chardonnay Sur Lie 66
Divinum Riesling 64
Dunavar "Connoisseur Collection" Pinot Gris 36
Gazela Vinho Verde 40
Gonzales Byass "Tio Pepe" Fino Sherry 138
Gray Monk "Odyssey" Pinot Gris 74
Hardys "Stamp Series" Riesling-Gewürztraminer 41
Lillet 137
Little Penguin Chardonnay 48
Lustau "Los Arcos" Dry Amontillado Sherry 136
Mad Dogs and Englishmen Monastrell-Shiraz-Cabernet Sauvignon 110